Lincoln

A LOS ANGELES QUAKES HOCKEY SERIES
BOOK ONE

ALISA JEAN

Lincoln: A Los Angeles Quakes Hockey Series, Book 1

Copyright © 2025 by Alisa Jean

All rights reserved.

Email: AlisaJean.author@gmail.com

No part of this work may be used, stored, reproduced, or transmitted without written permission from the author/publisher except for brief quotations for review purposes as permitted by law. Without in any way limiting the author's (and publisher's) exclusive rights under copyright, any use of this publication to "train" generative artificial intelligence (AI) technologies, in accordance with Article 4(3) of the Digital Single Market Directive 2019/790, to generate text is expressly prohibited. The author reserves all right to license uses of this work for generative AI training and development of machine learning language models.

This book is licensed for your personal enjoyment only. This book may not be re-sold or given away to other people. If you would like to share this book with another person, please purchase an additional copy for the recipient. If you're reading this book and did not purchase it, or it was not purchased for your use only, please purchase your own copy. Thank you for respecting the hard work of this author.

This book is a work of fiction. Names, characters, businesses, places, events, locales, and incidents are either products of the author's imagination or used in a fictitious manner. Any resemblance to actual persons, living or dead, or actual events is entirely coincidental.

Cover Design: C J Bahr

cjbahr.author@gmail.com

❦ Created with Vellum

To the Jeskes
Thank you for sharing the fun, excitement, and love of NHL hockey.
#GoKingsGo

CHAPTER
One

LINCOLN

Sweat drips into my eye. I shake my head, clearing the biting drops as I peer around the hulking body of an opposing team member, trying to find the puck. The shot is coming, I can feel it, but there are too many bodies in front of my crease. Hearing the crack of a puck on stick, I instinctively lunge left, raising my glove above my shoulder. A split second later, the biscuit pings off and caroms away. *Hot damn*! A save. The sound of the fans' roar inside the arena vibrates through my chest as their chants of "Go Quakes Go" grow louder. Luka Ribic, our hot left winger, picks the puck clear, but his pass to our captain, Zach Hansson, gets intercepted. A Seattle Sting Ray steals the black disc and skates into the neutral zone to reset. This penalty kill, with four of my guys playing against five of the Rays while one of our D-men does his time in the sin bin, drags on forever.

Head on a swivel, I track the puck ping-ponging between Stinger players. My teammates try clearing the puck from our zone, but it isn't happening. A Sting Ray sweeps behind my goal, hoping to sneak one past me, but I grant him no joy as I stick poke the rubber disc away. My luck runs foul when the puck ricochets off a skate blade, bouncing to center ice onto the stick of our opponent. Without hesitating, he snaps his wrist and slaps the disc toward the top right corner. Caught at the wrong side of the pipes, I throw myself, glove and leg stretching, yet it sails a thread's width from my hand and into the back of the net. *Fuck!*

The red light flashes, and the buzzer sounds. The crowd grows hushed except for the small number of Seattle fans. I stand and grab my water bottle resting on the outside of my net in the backside cupholder. The cold water hits the back of my throat. Refreshing, but it does nothing for my mood. I slam the bottle back where it's safe from the game and settle inside my crease.

The teams reset at center ice for another faceoff. The score is three-four, with two minutes and twenty seconds left in the third period. Yeah, we're screwed. My teammates will fight like hell, to tie and send the game into overtime. We'd at least get a point, maybe even win, but the chances are against us. But then again, we've scored in the last few seconds of games before either tying or winning, earning us the nickname—the *Aftershocks*. Sticks cross. I need the win, as does my team.

The referee drops the puck, and Zach wins the faceoff. He sends it floating between a Sting Ray's legs to hit the Quakes' defenseman, Eddie Landry's stick. He jukes and pivots in a fake-out before passing to Connor D'Angelo. Our right-winger snipes a one-timer at the Stinger's goal, but the goalie smothers the puck in his glove, stopping the play.

A glance at the clock shows seventy seconds left, and then my gaze shoots to the bench. Coach should pull me for an empty net to get an extra forward on the ice, especially since we're not in our zone and losing. A definite shake of his head keeps me in the crease. Our team switches lines for another faceoff but at the right-hand circle in the offensive zone. Jake

Novak, the center for our third line, wins the puck. D-man Alex Bouchard snatches it and wings the puck around the boards behind the net. Andre Forsberg is there to receive, but a Stinger slams him into the boards with a questionable hit. An opposing teammate shoots the puck, sending it my way.

No way in hell am I allowing an icing to stop the play. I skate out of my crease to intercept. Spotting Eddie, I send the puck his way. He doesn't hesitate and skates hard for neutral ice and into the offensive zone. A quick pass to Zach, who's back on the ice and snipes the puck from center ice, but a Seattle Sting Ray throws his body in sacrifice, blocking the shot. Luka snatches the rebound and pivots. With a fiery backhand, he shoots at the goal. The puck sails through the air. The Quakes' fans are standing on their feet, screaming, and then the puck hits the crossbar and pings away.

The end-game horn blares through the arena. *Fuck me.* Another loss with me between the pipes.

X

"So, do you think Alexandr Dvorak should have played tonight?" I overhear a reporter asking Luka Ribic, one of tonight's scorers. With his *GQ* looks, fans have voted him the best-looking player in the Pacific Coast division three years running, as well as making it to the All-Star team twice. It would be easy to hate him if he wasn't one of my best friends. "After all, Cavanaugh has lost the last five when he's been in net."

I flinch, and my hands clench, not wanting to hear Luka's answer, but in a sick way, I can't stop eavesdropping. It's not like it's hard to catch, since Ribi is only two cubbies away.

"Did you notice the twenty-three saves Caveman stopped? He saved our asses. The Stingers' score would have been ridiculous without our veteran in the crease. Sure, Dvorak is playing hot right now, but the Quakes lose or win as a team. We could have blocked more shots out there, but we didn't."

Having heard enough and appreciating Luka's support, I grab my towel and head for the showers. Last year, I had an amazing season with a .923 average, placing me among the top ten goalies in the entire league. Now, I'm not even in the top twenty-five. Crossing through the locker room, I'm careful to ensure my stride is even. No way I will allow any hint of weakness to show, especially with the reporters here.

Inside the shower room, I go to the farthest glass-partitioned stall and turn on the water, waiting for the spray to heat. Normally, one of the unwritten rules is first in, turn on all the showers so your teammates don't have to wait for hot water, but living in drought country, that's a no-go. I step beneath the showerhead, letting the lukewarm blast stream down my body. Bowing my head, I press my hands to the white tile and try to breathe.

Everything hurts, but the most worrisome is my hip. Two seasons ago, I had a hip impingement, suffering a labral tear. Instantaneous pain laid me out on the ice with fiery hot spikes shooting me in the groin. I had to be helped to the locker room because I couldn't stand on my own. The injury had required surgery, but luckily, or unluckily, depending on your point of view, I only missed four games. The Quakes were bounced out of the playoffs in round one—not even making it to game seven. I religiously worked on my rehab, entered the next season stronger than ever, and became one of the top goalies in the league.

Fast forward to this year's training camp, and while fighting to prove I deserved the top goalie spot, I felt a twinge in the previously injured area. When the season started, the intermittent pain shooting from my hip to my groin disappeared with careful stretching and a ton of ice. Until tonight. I sigh and start shampooing, beginning my ritual of getting clean. I needed a fucking win. Losing five games when in net has never happened to me before. So when the puck shot toward the opposite side of the crease, I threw my leg out, and something popped. I refuse to be injured. There may be no coming back this time.

After rinsing off, I wrap my towel around my waist. My teammates had entered while I'd been lost in my thoughts. I concentrate on keeping my gait even, shoulders square, and head held high as I leave the showers. I know the smart thing to do would be to join Anzor, the only player older than me, in the ice baths, but I can't let on to anyone—especially the med staff—that I might be injured. The freezing bath will have to wait until I get home, which shit, means stopping at the store for the usual twenty-five pounds of ice. Might as well get another mega-sized bottle of ibuprofen while I'm at it.

Some guys must have beaten me out of the showers while I woolgathered because when I enter the locker room, several players are already dressed. Not engaging with my teammates' banter and baiting, I head straight to my cubicle, glad I don't have to avoid stepping on the Quakes' logo centered on the floor. Ours is on the ceiling, making the hockey superstition obsolete. Because walking on the mat is bad luck, and since mine sucks lately, I'm happy not to jinx the team.

I drop my towel and pull on a set of boxer briefs, my back to the room.

"Thank the lucky hockey gods tomorrow is a day off," Andre Forsberg throws out. "Coach would have kicked our asses on the ice if we had practice. As sure as shit, I'm thankful he doesn't believe in bag skates."

The room groans. They used to use the drill of sprinting from goal line to goal and back again in fast bursts. Luckily, that particular hellish abuse pretty much disappeared in pro hockey.

"Bergie," Cory Fournier raises his hand, drawing the right-winger's attention. "I may be new to this team, but even

I know Coach will make us his bitches next skate, with or without a bag."

Chuckles filter through my teammates because he isn't wrong, and we all know it. Cory is a great addition to the team. The Ottawa Heralds traded him for the Quakes' second-draft pick. Foursie has solidified our second line and brought humor and joy to our game with his self-deprecating personality. Plus, the guy can skate and find the back of the net, which he did again tonight. He now has twenty-eight points with his goals and assists in thirty-four games played this season.

"Bakes!" Mikey Cote shouts to our rookie defenseman. "That was an outstanding hard hit on Richardson. Proud of you, man, our baby Quake taking on the Stingers' captain."

The room cheers and disperses fist bumps for Sean Baker, our new twenty-year-old acquisition. The kid played an amazing game with short ice time.

Eddie Landry, veteran D-man and alternate captain, slaps Sean on the back. "First beer at MacKay's is on me, Bakes."

"Hey, we can hook him up with his first puck bunny," Trevor Rayne, third-line blue liner and the team's man whore, suggests. "He deserves a reward."

"You know who doesn't deserve a reward? Cavanaugh. Coach better put Dvorak in net next game. I'm sick of losing." Matthew Holt, a defenseman and all-around douchebag, gripes. I ignore him and keep dressing.

"Shit, Holt," Brian Anderson, veteran forward, and one of my closest friends, defends me. "If it hadn't been for your penalty, we wouldn't have been a man down in a PK."

"I tripped that Seattle asshole to stop a play. All Cave had to do was catch the biscuit. It's his job. But no, another puck in the net and a loss to a team we should have beaten." Holt throws his shower kit hard into the cubby. "For fuck's sake, Seattle is one of the shittiest teams in the Pacific League—"

"Enough," Zach, ever the captain and peacemaker, interrupts Holt's rant. "We play as a team and lose as a team."

"Funny how we win as a team with Raki in the crease." Holt grabs his wallet, phone, and keys. "Just speaking the harsh truth. I'm out of here, fuckers." And on that cheery note, he struts out of the locker room.

I plop my ass on the seat of my cubicle and run my hand through my damp hair, closing my eyes. My groin and hip are throbbing, I'm depressed, and I can't even make the argument that Holt's wrong. Maybe I should retire. I'm thirty-six. A handful of hockey players continue to their forties, but those are the special cases, and most aren't net minders. I helped the Quakes win two Stanley Cups. I fucking love hockey. What the hell will I do if I can't play?

"Hey," a hushed voice draws my attention, causing me to open my eyes. Brian is crouched next to me. He reaches out a hand and squeezes my shoulder. "Are you all right?"

I shrug, causing Bri's hand to fall. What is there to say? I'm nowhere near fine, but I'm not about to open up and talk about all this shit swirling around in my head. Call it living up to my "Caveman" nickname, but it's just not how I'm built. I'd rather put my fist through a wall. Thankfully, Luka exits the shower at that moment, later than the rest of the team, because of his multiple interviews. He takes one look around, notices the mostly empty room and the grim expressions on the remaining players' faces.

"What the hell happened?" Luka stares hard at Brian and me. "Everything was fine. I leave to shower, then *bam*, all the sad and worried faces."

"Holt happened," Jake Novak calls out. "See you guys at MacKay's." He hurries out, knowing when to leave. All that's left is me and my core group of close friends.

"Linc, you know Holt is an asshole." Brian draws my attention away from Jakie's fleeing figure. "Yeah, he's *our* asshole, but just the same, he had no right to speak to you that way."

Zach wanders over. "Listen to Bri. You are a valuable member of this team."

I make myself meet his gaze. "Honestly? I'm not so sure…" I can't finish. Saying it out loud feels final, and I'm not ready to throw in the towel yet.

"Stop that shit, here and now," Zach demands. "You're my friend and my teammate. You are not the reason we're losing games."

"Um, yeah, I am. If the puck gets past me, those points on the board are on me. No one else."

"Bullshit," Luka adds his two cents as he dresses. "Our team is letting you down. We need to block more, making those saves and even sacrificing our bodies to stop pucks. Not only our D-men but all the forwards as well."

I shake my head, and Zach glares.

"Linc, listen to me. You are a veteran and mentor. You are essential to this team."

"Am I, Zach? Because Holt's right. The team plays better with Raki in goal. The proof is right there in our stats."

"No, man." Brian raises a hand in protest. "We're a team. It's not one player who tanks the squad."

I sigh. I love my friends, but we're talking in circles. The Quakes win when Alexandr Dvorak is net-minding, so the conclusion is pretty obvious. The problem is me.

"Enough of this." Zach grabs my arm and hauls me to my feet. "We're going to MacKay's and getting you some beers." I sputter a protest, but he stops me with a glare. "Ribi, are you about done? All the primping in the world isn't gonna help you."

"Yeah, yeah, asshole. I'm ready." Luka joins our group.

My friends close ranks around me. Not sure if they are being supportive, or if they are keeping me from escaping. They must sense I have absolutely no desire to hang out at the team's watering hole. Holt isn't the only one trash-talking. I'm taking a beating on social media. Our fans can be ruthless. After another loss, all I want is to go home and have a beer while sitting in my homemade ice bath, praying I haven't fuckered myself.

Yet, best friends are friends for a reason. They worry about me and don't want me to be alone. Also, the guys refuse to let me hide, even though it's what I want deep inside.

Luka bumps my shoulder. "Cavie, it's gonna be okay."

I don't reply. It isn't necessary, because we all know it might not be. But for a little while, I'm dumping my concerns and hanging with my boys tonight, setting in to forget.

CHAPTER Two

CATHERINE

I arrive at our practice arena, which also houses our executive offices. When you share a sports arena with an NBA team, the people who manage and run both teams have to go elsewhere to work. Hence, the drive to El Segundo. I pull into an empty parking spot near the front. There are plenty of spots to choose from since it's early. Just a handful of cars are in the lot.

As I lock my ice-silver metallic Subaru BRZ, my phone dings. Ugh, who wants me now? It's seven in the morning, the day after a game. Can't people bug me during normal business hours? I may be the heir-apparent for the Los Angeles Quakes, but no one else seems to care. Well, except for my dad, Robert Bishop, the current owner of the Quakes. Though, let's be honest, his idea of *grooming* me for taking over isn't easy, either. But I don't care, because I love it. Hockey is in my blood. I can't wait to be the first female owner of an NHL team. One of my earliest memories is sitting on my dad's lap, watching a game together. As the years roll on, I still hang with my father and take in games in person when we can and on TV when we can't. It's our thing.

I grab my phone, unlock the screen, and start heading into the office. There's a text from my younger brother, Josh, who works in the marketing department for the Quakes.

> Josh: Hey big sis, r u @ wrk?

> Me: Here now, walking in.

> Josh: Me, 2! Need 2 shw u smthg.

What the hell is he doing here already? He's not the workaholic that I am. Plus, it's too early to decipher Josh's texts. I'm not that much older than he is, but according to him, I text like our father. Full words and punctuation. So sue me. I take my education seriously. There were private schools, Ivy League Universities, and an MBA degree from Wharton's at the end. I refuse to butcher the English language. Sometimes, trying to figure out a Josh text takes higher brain function and coffee. Lots of coffee. I need a caffeine fix. Especially when I'm reading, texting, and walking at the same time.

I glance away from my phone when I reach the entrance, long enough to pull open the door, walk through, and let it shut behind me before texting him back.

> Me: Busy today. Tomorrow?

> Josh: No! Tmrw is Sat. Pls?

> Me: Let me check my schedule when I get to my office.

> Josh: Thks. Ur best!!

I turn the corner while slipping my phone into my purse when I collide with a muscled wall. Gasping, I stumble but am prevented from falling on my ass by two firm hands gripping my shoulders, steadying me. My head snaps up.

Lincoln Cavanaugh. Oh. My. God. I gaze into his steel-gray eyes, frozen. I used to see him at the team events and parties Dad would throw at the house. But that was before I left for college, back when I was a gawky teen. This is the closest I have been to my secret crush since I grew up. More specifically, filled out my curves. Our bodies are inches apart, and I'm flustered. The temporary paralysis wears off, and I splutter an apology.

"Oh, my gosh. I'm so sorry. I should have looked where I was going instead of nearly running you down."

He chuckles, low and warm. "I doubt you would have taken me out."

He has a point. I'm tall for a woman. In bare feet, I'm five-foot-eight, and right now, I'm wearing three-inch heels, and yet his six-foot-four frame makes me feel petite.

"Probably not." I nervously laugh. We're still standing close, and I realize he hasn't removed his hands, which are resting on me. Not that I mind. Many a night in college, I fantasized about having his hands on my body. "Hey, sorry for the tough loss. I thought you made some amazing saves. The players need to stop hanging you out to dry."

Some expression I can't read flits across his handsome face before he drops his hold and steps back. *Damn*. Not the smartest or smoothest move, mentioning the loss. I plant my high-heeled foot in my mouth. When will I stop being such a flustered idiot around him?

"Yeah, maybe." Linc shrugs his wide shoulders. "I should, ah, let you go. I'm sure you're busy. It was nice running into you, Ms. Bishop."

"Ha, I think that's my line," I offer him a smile. "And it's Catherine." All the players know they can call me by my first name. My father and I like to keep things informal so the team finds us approachable. We want them to come to us if there's a problem and not feel threatened by titles or formalities. "Wait," a sudden thought crosses my mind. "What are you doing here? Isn't today your day off? Nothing's wrong, is there?"

He shakes his head. "Ah, no, Ms—Catherine. No problem. I snuck in an extra workout."

"But you're supposed to rest. That's the whole point of an off day," I protest. "Your body needs recovery time."

"All the players do it." He gives a sheepish smile. "Especially when we've reached the middle of the season and want to keep or better our playoff position."

"I guess I can keep the players' secret. Whatever you do, don't let Coach O'Ryan or my dad find out."

His smile grows, revealing a dimple, making me hold my breath. Dear God, he is stunning. With those mischievous eyes, dark hair I want to run my fingers through, a strong jaw, full lips, and angled cheekbones, Lincoln Cavanaugh could be a model. Oh, wait, he is. I remember the high-end watch campaign he modeled as the spokesperson in a mouthwatering ad. That was a few years ago, but time has only made him more handsome.

"I don't think we players are hiding anything from them." He winks and steps around me, heading toward the entrance. "Have a good day, Ms. Bishop."

"It's Catherine," I growl as I watch him leave. Lincoln chuckles. Good Lord, his ass is amazing in those faded jeans. The rear view is almost as tasty as the front. He reaches the door and exits, disappearing from my lustful gaze, happy he didn't catch me ogling him. I give myself a shake and walk deeper into the facility.

There is a purpose for my early arrival. I need to get some work done before the nine o'clock meeting with my father. This leaves me plenty of time to get through my emails and check the prospects and trade reports. We're heading into the official holiday break, but the trade deadline is a little more than two months away. It's never too soon to plan for what's best for the team. And I refuse to be caught off guard in front of Geoffrey Carter, our general manager. Reading the reports and staying in the loop have served me well in dealing with our misogynistic GM. It could be he hates me because he knows I'll clean house when I'm in charge. Geoffrey Carter treats women horribly. He's hitting on us, making insensitive comments, or treating us like we have low IQs and we should all be secretaries. Not executive assistants. Lord, no. That title is too glorious for the little ladies who should be seen and not heard.

I open my office door, mentally preparing a to-do list of everything I need to accomplish.

"Catherine."

I flinch when I hear Geoffrey's voice. Think of the devil, and he shall appear. *Dammit*. What is he doing here so early? Is everyone getting a jumpstart on their day? Plastering a pleasant expression on my face, I slowly turn and watch him stride toward me. He once was an NHL player, but where many former players keep their fighting form, not so much with Carter. You'd never know he used to be a professional athlete. He's a mundane aging white man—balding, slight beer-belly, and thinks he rules the world. I remember meeting him for the first time twenty-three years ago. My dad, as the new owner of the Los Angeles Quakes, hosted a welcome party for the entire team. The invite included everyone—players, coaches, trainers, staff, and management. I was only seven, but the day is clear in my memories. After all, this was my first time I got to meet professional hockey players in person. I had stars in my eyes.

My father introduced the family to Geoffrey. He was the assistant GM at the time and was quick to mask his shock when he realized the beautiful Black woman standing next to my dad was his wife. Robert Bishop had met his future wife when he was in Cape Town, South Africa, working a business deal. According to him, it was love at first sight, but not so much for my mom, Amahle Khoza. However, Robert Bishop hadn't become one of the youngest billionaires in the world without tenacity. It had taken him almost a month for her to agree to a date and then, a year later, to put a ring on her finger. They had a brief engagement before Amahle became Khoza-Bishop.

Even at seven, as a child of mixed race, I knew that quickly shuttered expression on Carter's face all too well. Later, I caught him staring in disgust at my parents from across the room. Obviously, he had a problem with interracial couples. He hates me, and I can't stand him. I haven't spoken with my dad about Geoff's behavior and not-so-subtle racism. Maybe it's time? But my father believes in loyalty, and no matter my personal feelings, Carter has built the Quakes into multiple Cup champions. Too bad he comes in a bigoted, misogynistic package.

"Geoffrey, you're in early."

"I need to speak to you." He gestures into my office. "This isn't a conversation for the hallway."

Shrugging, I walk into the office and head for my desk. He shuts the door with a bang and stops my progress by grabbing my arm. I glare at his hand, but he doesn't remove it. I try to tug out of his grip, but that only makes him tighten his hold.

"I would remove your hand if you want to speak with me."

He grimaces but lets me go. "This is important, Catherine."

"Which doesn't excuse the manhandling." I straighten my shoulders and face him squarely. No way will I let him intimidate me. "What do you want?"

"You and me, we've got to be on the same page during the meeting."

I frown. I thought this morning's appointment was

between my dad and me. Before I can speak, Carter blathers on.

"We're going to discuss Cavanaugh, and you *will* back me."

"What about Lincoln?" An alarm bell goes off in my head since this meeting was to discuss possible trades.

"I want him on waivers, so someone will take him off our hands or send him down to the AHL if no one claims him. Or fucking get him to retire by blaming an injury. I don't care. The Quakes need him gone. Today, if possible. He's dead weight and messing with our salary cap." Carter's hands clench into fists, and his face is turning red.

"Look, Geoffrey—"

"No, you look, missy. You'll do as you're told. You have no idea what it takes to manage a professional hockey team. Have my back, or you'll regret it." With those threatening and demeaning words, he storms out of my office.

Stunned, I stand there staring at my open door. What the hell just happened? I'm not shocked by his behavior. It's sort of par for the course. But it's a sad fact I kind of agree with him. Even though I'm crushing on our veteran goalie, it doesn't mean I can't be professional and separate my personal feelings for what's best for the business. I don't know what's happened to Lincoln's game, but it is shit right now, though not entirely his fault. Hockey is a team sport, and the players have been crap for him. If Dvorak becomes our number one, the Quakes need a more reliable and stable second, which isn't Lincoln at present.

Personally, I'll miss him if he's waivered or traded, but I have to think about what's best for the Quakes. I walk to my desk and plop down in the leather chair. Sometimes making the hard decisions sucks, especially when they're in line with the asshole GM. I wake my computer and get to work with a heavy mind.

From my seat on the couch next to my father, we watch Geoff leave. Our GM isn't thrilled at the moment. A sigh escapes me, and I shift on the sofa, facing Dad more directly.

"You know I'm not impressed with Carter."

Robert Bishop raises his hand, stopping me from continuing. "You realize you'll have to work out your differences when I finally retire."

I laugh. "No, I won't, because he won't be my GM."

"Catie, he's a strong general manager. He may be a bit of an asshole, but Geoffrey Carter has done an amazing amount of good for the Quakes. He's one of the best GMs this team has ever had. His biggest flaw is he's too quick to write people off, but that's why we're the ones to make the final decisions."

Shaking my head, I try again. "Listen, Dad. I kind of agree with him about Lincoln. You know the weight of this decision because I would disagree with Carter on anything just to piss him off. But we need strong goaltenders, and Lincoln isn't one at the moment."

Dad lovingly pats my shoulder. "My answer is still no. You know I value loyalty almost above all else. Linc is having a rough patch, but he'll get out of it. I'm not going to cut one of the league's best goalies over a couple of losses."

"Dad," I sigh.

"No, Catie-bug. I'm not tossing him away." He smiles. "Now, your mother is driving me crazy with this holiday party. I would appreciate it if you'd step in. Bishop Tech awaits no man, including me, CEO or not. This microchip deal must close by year's end. I've got enough on my plate without mulling if we have an adequate amount of live evergreen decorations to please the boss." He stands, and I follow suit. "Take the rest of today off and go to the house. Grab Josh while you're at it and put him to work."

"Of course, Dad."

He gives me a smile and hugs me. "If I see your older brother at Bishop Tech, I'll send him your way. I don't want you to think since you're female, you're doing the decorating. The boys can help as well."

"Sure. Though I think Daniel may be more of a liability than a help."

"Too true. Your mother sounds stressed, and I want her happy. Thank you for doing this." He kisses my cheek. "I'll try to be home early. It would be nice if we could have a family dinner. It's been a while since we've been under the same roof."

"Sounds like a plan."

We say goodbye and part in the hallway. He leaves for the parking lot, and I head to collect Josh. Our family is close. We're a team, and this squad is going to knock a rocking holiday party out of the park.

CHAPTER
Three

LINCOLN

I pull into the Bishop's circular driveway in my restored classic 1965 Rally Red convertible Corvette and wait in line for valet parking. Usually, I look forward to the annual holiday party. The Bishops open their doors to the team every year, cementing the notion that we're not just numbers to them but family. Only this year, I'm letting the family down. I feel like the black sheep who doesn't deserve to be there.

When it's my turn at the valet, I have to grit my teeth to avoid groaning in pain as I get out of the driver's seat. The groin soreness isn't improving as fast as I'd like, making me regret the low slung car for the first time in my life. I reluctantly hand my keys to a guy with far more of a gleam in his eye than I'm comfortable with and head inside.

Robert Bishop was already a self-made billionaire when he bought the Quakes about ten years before I started playing pro hockey. One of the things I like about the guy, the whole family, really, is that they don't feel the need to flaunt it. Their house is enormous, don't get me wrong, but it's not as overdone as some L.A. mansions can get. Even their holiday decorations are tasteful. Cheerful, but not as heavy-handed as my dad's. He's compelled to wrap his modest Minnesota home in so many strands of lights we blow a fuse at least once every holiday season. The decorations and thoughts of home are almost enough to lift me out of my funk, but not quite.

Then I see Catherine through the large open patio doors, standing on the deck outside chatting with someone I recognize as front office staff. Yeah, it's L.A., so it's no problem having the afternoon party outdoors. Well, it's an indoor/outdoor party with food and drinks flowing in several locations, but most of it spills out onto the deck and backyard. My mom called last night to say they got another six inches of snow. The weather was one of the toughest changes I had to deal with when I moved here. That and coming out of the AHL after only one season and making it to the bigs, playing in Commerce Stadium with twenty-thousand screaming fans cheering you on. The things they're yelling at and about me now aren't so great, but I learned a long time ago that fans could turn on a dime and try not to take it too personally.

What *is* personal is the smile Catherine flashes at me when she sees me come out to the deck and accept a beer from the bartender. I know she smiles like that at everyone, but ever since she returned from grad school and took an active role with the team, I've let myself imagine that she's saving a special smile for me. *God, is that pervy?* I've known her since she was a kid. Back then, our six-year age difference seemed insurmountable, yet not so much now. She's all woman, as evidenced by the way she fills out her dark green dress. Usually, she camouflages her body under boxy suits, although when she wears a skirt, there's no hiding those long legs. But today, she's dressed for the occasion. Even her wavy brown hair, which she usually wears in a bun, is loosely woven in a festive style that frames her face beautifully.

LINCOLN 21

She walks toward me, looking a lot more comfortable than I feel in my tailored suit. When you have my build, every suit has to be tailored, but it doesn't make the tie any less restricting. "Catherine, you look amazing," I greet her when she draws near.

"Linc, I'm so glad you could make it." She does that air kiss thing, and my cock jumps, electrified by her slightest touch. "I thought you were going back to see your family over the break."

I take a sip of my beer to ease the sudden dryness in my mouth and try to will the growing erection away. It doesn't work. Why would a woman like her even care whether or not I made it? "That had been the plan until a snowstorm nixed it. The break is too short to gamble with the weather. Besides, this party has become a holiday tradition. Of course, it wasn't quite the same the few years without you." I realize too late how that sounded and stumble through an explanation that I hope negates the sleazy factor. "For your parents, I mean. I know they missed you."

"God knows why," comments a younger man, who gives her a loving hug as he makes his way to the bar. He eschewed the required suit for a trendy sports coat, dress shirt, tailored pants, and a good-sized diamond stud in his ear. His mocha skin and wavy dark hair make it clear he's related to Catherine but damned if I can remember her brothers' names. There are only two of them, but I can barely remember my name with her standing this close. Her subtle scent of orange blossom and spice fills my lungs, distracting me.

Laughing, she comes to my rescue. "Josh, you remember Lincoln Cavanaugh, our goalie? Linc, this is my younger brother, Josh. He works in our marketing department."

"Did you ask him yet?" the slight young man demands.

"Not yet, thanks for smashing through my pitch and getting down to it." Her tone is playful, but I can't help but feel disappointed. So this wasn't a social thing? She came to talk to me about business. At least I don't have to worry about that awkward bulge in my pants as my half-chub wilts.

She links her arm through mine and walks me in the opposite direction of the table laden with food. Even without Josh trailing on our heels, I now know this isn't about getting naked with each other. Because from the moment she walked toward me until her brother threw a bucket of cold water on my fantasy, that's all I'd been thinking about.

"Josh is working with Adidas on next season's annual retro jersey, and he's come up with an awesome design. You know, how everyone in the league is paying homage to their past. He showed me the design the other day, and it's kind of cool bringing back the old purple, gold, and white. But he really wants a player's input since you guys have to wear them, and you're more familiar with the old sweaters than anyone else."

The muscle in my jaw jumps of its own accord. "You mean because you think I'm one of the few players old enough to have worn the original sweater?" I know she didn't mean it that way, but it's the truth all the same. I unlink my arm from hers. "Sorry, I'm not quite *that* old. You'd have better luck asking Coach or Geoff Carter. They were on the team back when they wore those colors. If you'll excuse me, I see Sonny and his wife over by the pool. I'm going to go say hi. Merry Christmas to both of you if I don't see you before then."

I strut toward my linemate before either Bishop sibling can say anything. It was stupid to think Catherine wanted to talk about anything outside of team business with me. The woman's a genius with an Ivy League MBA. I'm the son of a blue-collar family from the mid-west who beat the odds and made it to the NHL. What other topics would we have in common other than hockey? Still, as irrational as it was, I thought I saw a gleam in her eye when we literally ran into each other in the lobby the other day. My thoughts are written all over my face because Sonny points a finger at me.

"What's with the grimace? I saw you smiling at Catherine a minute ago. What happened?"

"Did her younger brother cock block you?" Ribi jokes as he joins our little cluster.

Heat flushes up my neck and creeps toward my face. They hit closer to home than they could have guessed. "Ha ha, hilarious," I snark back as I exchange my now empty beer for another one at the poolside bar. Because yes, the Bishops have two bars outside and one inside. My place is nice, with a yard and a built-in BBQ and fridge, but it isn't two bartenders big. "No, the brother, Josh, is working on a retro jersey for the team and wanted to ask my opinion."

"On clothes?" Luka asks, laughing. "Has he seen your wardrobe? You only own this suit and tie because Jenny picked it out for you. You can barely pull together jeans and a shirt without a fashion disaster."

Yeah, clothes aren't my thing, not like Luka, who's a fashion hound. Most of my teammates haven't figured out my secret. Being color-blind sucks. So I hide it by being deliberately fashion awkward. It's not hard to fake it when it's real. My boys know, and Jenny, Sonny's wife, hence my tie matching my suit tonight. Also, there's my family. I get tons of fashion help from my mom and sisters. We've got a code worked out. They buy me stuff, which, of course, I reimburse them for, and they inscribe a Sharpie mark on the label. It helps me figure out what to pair with what. *Garanimals*, adult style. It's not perfect, especially when I forget to refresh the code mark after multiple washings. So, being known as fashionably challenged is a plus in my book.

"You're a regular Jerry Seinfeld, aren't you?" I growl back at him. Normally, I don't mind a little ribbing, and I sure as shit don't care if I meet anyone's fashion approval. But I can't get the soft warmth of Catherine's lips brushing my cheek out of my head, and it's making me cranky.

"Jesus, even the comedians you pick are old," Matt Holt

snorts. He and Sean Baker, our young rookie, join our conversation for what reason God only knows. Holt has to realize we all think he's an asshole, right? "Yeah, I heard about this retro thing. I figured they'd come to you since you probably knitted the original sweaters, *Caveman*."

Sean lets out a guffaw that's cut short when he realizes no one else is laughing. He doesn't understand what a poor choice it is hanging with Holtie, but he'll figure it out when the invites for beers after the game aren't as exuberant as they were after the last one. Holt's such a sarcastic dick he's no fun to be around, especially when you're the target of his jokes. Besides, Matt will push the kid away because, God forbid, Holt, the isolating, angry bastard, will have friends.

The muscles in my arms clench, and my hand curls into a fist, but my brain takes over just in time. This fancy party with the Bishops and their rich friends in attendance, jonesing to hang out with pro athletes, is not the time or the place. Out of the corner of my eye, I see Sonny let out a sigh of relief. One side of his mouth curls up in an *I got you* expression, and he nods back.

Unfortunately, Holt just keeps talking.

"I know the league goes retro"—he makes annoying air quotes—"but hasn't it gone on long enough? It has to be some owner's wife or daughter who wants to keep it going. I mean, how stupid, right? Styles go out for a reason."

Jenny stiffens. "Are you seriously saying that it had to be a woman's doing because a man never has a dumb idea?"

Silence falls over our little group, and, shit, Zach can't step in. His wife would kick him out of their bed for a month for assuming she can't handle an idiot like Holt, but if he doesn't, Holt will call him a pussy. Fortunately, just like on the ice, Andre Forsberg steps in to have his teammate's back.

"Okay, everybody, chill out. *Smaken är som baken*— different strokes for different folks. It's a Christmas party, remember? Peace on fucking earth and goodwill toward men, even Holtie. Who wants to come with me and see the kids play in the snow?" The big Swede smiles at the group.

Yes, snow. The Bishops had a company dump a ton of snow in another part of the backyard so the little kids can make snow angels and snowmen. It's pretty adorable, especially seeing the ones who have never been in the snow react. So sure, I'm in. I follow Bergie, Sonny, and Jenny when I hear Holt get in one last dig.

"God help us if the rumors are true, and old man Bishop gives the team to his daughter instead of one of the boys. Everybody knows women don't understand sports. They're just too soft." I stop in my tracks, and Baker's laugh dies in his throat. It takes Zach a few steps to realize I'm no longer following them. I haven't changed course, just stopped walking, so I see his shoulders slump before he turns back.

"Linc, it's seriously not worth it."

I cock an eyebrow at him. *Isn't it, though?* Because I've been here a lot longer than Matt, I know Catherine is a hockey fanatic. Loves it, played it, and is smart. Everything she's ever suggested has been calculating, almost coldly so. She's on track to being the first woman to own a hockey team, and I think that's great. I don't care what equipment the owner is using. I just want to play the game.

The sons are okay, I guess, but their disinterest in hockey is obvious. Maybe it's some Freudian daddy-issue thing. Maybe they're just jealous of the connection Catherine and Robert share over it, who knows? That's way above my pay grade. All I know is Josh, the one in marketing, is more into selling the team to the public, boosting our image than actual plays on the ice. Daniel, the oldest, makes terrible choices in everything he does. From business partners who have exaggerated the value of their product to wives he picks for the wrong reason, he can't seem to catch a break. Or, if what my dad says is true, and a man makes his own luck, Daniel is pretty shitty at it. One season with him at the helm and the

Quakes would be in the basement with no ladder to get us out.

"Sorry, man," I say to Zach before pivoting to where Matt stands at the bar. I poke him hard in the chest, making him stumble backward a little. Not enough to land on his ass, but I got his attention. I've got a couple of inches of height on him, but he outweighs me by fifteen pounds, and it's all muscle. On the ice, where footwork matters, I could take him easily, but on terra firma? This might not have been the smartest move I've ever made, but it felt good.

"Oh, you want a piece of this, old man?" Holt rushes forward and plows into me. He uses his size well, but he's had a few more drinks than me, so it's easy to sidestep and use his momentum against him. It works, but it's likely a mistake he won't make again. He rears back, taking a swing at me, when I hear someone shout my name. It sounds like a woman, but I'm too focused on setting my return hit to look. Fortunately, the other guys swarm us and come between the little shit and me. I honestly don't know who would have won, and we have too many players on injured reserve to risk either of us getting hurt, but for the first time since that fifth loss, I feel pretty fucking young.

CHAPTER
Four

CATHERINE

"Linc," I shout, seeing the fight break out near the pool. Dad shoots me a look, a satisfied smirk on his face. "What? Those idiots are brawling in the middle of our holiday party."

"I know. It would be a shame if one of them got hurt."

"Those fools deserve what they get, but they're ruining the party," I huff. Only that's not the point. It's hard enough to watch Linc play—don't get me wrong, it's exciting and thrilling and so hot—but even with helmets and padding on, they have carted players off the ice unmoving. If Holt broke Linc's beautiful nose or knocked out a tooth, I'd kill him.

"Sweetheart, it's fine," my mother gestures to the guests who are closing in to watch the shit storm. "Apparently, our guests are finding it entertaining."

"Wonder what that's all about?" Dad muses, curious. I've known my whole life that he thinks of the players as his extended family and truly cares if something is bothering one of them. Compared to him, sometimes I think I'm Attila the

Hun. I don't want to get so attached that I can't make the tough calls for the sake of the team.

"Probably Holt, giving him a hard time about his age. Linc seems touchy about that these days." I feel like such an idiot at the way Josh and I so thoughtlessly pitched him on the idea of giving his input on the retro jerseys. Of course, we didn't mean it like that, but I should have been more sensitive.

"Why don't you go down there, hon, and try to cool Linc off?"

"Me?" I squeak, embarrassed at the way my voice jumps an octave. How am I supposed to look him in the eye and tell him age is only a number or some other bullshit when I'm the one lobbying to trade him?

"Yes, you. I saw you two talking earlier. I think if he'll listen to anyone, it's you." Taking my glass of wine out of my hands, he gives me a little push. "Hurry now, before things get out of hand. We don't want to see our whole bench out in the backyard tearing each other apart."

Walking across the yard is tricky wearing heels, so I take them off and stride out to where the fistfight had devolved into the two would-be gladiators snarling and spitting at each other over the massive bodies of their teammates, keeping them apart. I take a stand on neutral ground between the two masses of people, already tired of having to look up at them without my heels. My only comfort is that both of my brothers are about my height, so they would have had no height advantage either.

"Boys, anyone want to tell me why a bar fight broke out during my Christmas party?"

"No, ma'am," Linc mumbles while Holt grunts in reply. Which tells me it was about the age thing. I understand he's young and dumb, but Holt would be lucky to be Linc's age and still play. That's something to be respected, not mocked. Time is a cruel master to us all. "I believe we've all had enough entertainment for the night. Perhaps, gentlemen, you should go to your separate corners, please."

Matt gives another grunt and walks into the house, straight to the bar. Turning to face Linc, I catch him mid-pivot, see his shoulder hunch, and he freezes. Did he get hurt in the fight? Stalking closer, I catch his parting words to the players still hovering.

"I think I'm all partied out, guys. I'm going to go home."

Luka steps forward. "Come on, man. Don't let that asshole chase you away."

"He's right." I step to Linc's side. "Don't go home. I have a better idea."

He throws a glance my way, and I can see he's still pissed. At Holt, or maybe me? "What?" His single-word question is growly, but at least I have his attention.

"MacKay's. I've never been to the team's hangout."

"Excellent suggestion." Luka agrees and slaps Linc's shoulder. "Both brains and beauty. Let's move the party."

I can tell Linc isn't happy, but he nods anyway. And before I know it, several players and I gather around the valet, waiting for the cars to arrive.

The drive from Holmby Hills to downtown Los Angeles takes a surprisingly short amount of time. A holiday miracle. As was Lincoln's offer to drive me.

I had been about to get into Zach's SUV with his wife when he opened the passenger door of his shiny red vintage Corvette and called my name. To tell the truth, his offer shocked me, considering I thought he was mad at me, but I didn't hesitate to accept. As soon as I was belted in, he reached for the radio and turned on a classic rock station. I took the hint. He's not in a chatty mood.

Thank God the ride downtown is faster than normal. I've never been good with awkward silence, and this is killing me. I can't figure out a way to apologize, so I keep my mouth shut for once instead of putting my foot in it again.

We pull into an industrial parking lot, and Linc finds a spot and stops. He turns off the radio and the rumble of the muscle car's engine. He sits there for a moment before facing me.

"Sorry for the silent treatment. I needed some time to get out of my head."

"No, I'm sorry. The retro jersey thing came out all wrong—"

He holds up a hand and shakes his head, stopping my babble. "It's fine. I've been in a shit mood lately and shouldn't have taken it out on you."

"Linc."

He shakes his head again and smirks. "Let's stop the apology carousel and get a beer. Come on, let me show you the Quakes' watering hole."

We exit and meet at the front of the Corvette. His hand lands on the small of my back as he guides me toward the large warehouse ahead. I flush from the contact, which burns me through the silk of my dress. My crush is touching me, and I shiver.

Linc's head swivels in my direction. "Cold?"

"N-no, I'm good."

"Sure? I can give you my jacket."

"Nope. Maybe later."

He faces forward and gestures with his free hand. "Welcome to MacKay's."

The brewery bar has an indoor/outdoor vibe that only warm climate cities can achieve, starting with the three wide cargo bay doors of the warehouse pulled open. They scattered picnic tables throughout the large outdoor area in front of the building, currently filled with people. Some are eating and drinking, others are playing games like cornhole, the giant-size Jenga, and even board games. Inside the warehouse, they have more tables and some booths, as well as a wall of dartboards. In the far back of the building, there are huge vats I'm sure are the microbrewery part.

The bar is lively with an open vibe, and the players fit right in. They sign some autographs and take selfies as they enter, but the fans back off and leave them alone when they make their way to a cluster of tables outside in the corner marked as reserved.

I feel bad when none of the fans approach Lincoln, no doubt not helping his mood. He guides me to the team's tables and the open spot near Zach, his wife Jenny, Luka, Brian, and Andre Forsberg.

"Ms. Bishop, you remember my wife, Jenny?" he says in that lovely Swedish accent.

"Of course." I offer her a welcoming smile.

"Ma'am, nice to meet you again." Her twang is a giveaway that he met her in the States. From the solid grip when we shake hands, I'm betting Texas.

"Last one here, you have to get the beers," Andre shouts. "And you drove a 'Vette. How the hell did that happen?"

"Precious cargo, idiot." My insides warm, and my skin tingles from his comment. He drove safely for me. Sigh. He turns to me. "Pale, medium, or dark? What kind of beer do you drink?"

"Um, amber?" I'm not a huge beer drinker, but it better be a good one if I do.

"Get her a *Lucky Penny*," Jenny suggests.

As Lincoln makes his way inside, I realize he might need help carrying everyone's drink. I stand. "I should help since I'm the reason we're last."

Zach stops me with a hand on my arm. "Sit. He's only

placing an order. They'll bring the drinks to us since there are so many. Plus, it's easier not to get mobbed by the fans while trapped at the bar, though they usually are pretty respectful." I plop down. "Besides, you're in our hangout. Your drinks are on us."

"If you say so." I smile at the players, who all have lost their suit coats and ties, looking relaxed and happy. Glancing around, I realize how overdressed I am and sigh. Unlike the men, Jenny and I are stuck in our fancy dresses along with the players who have plus ones here. Oh well, no one seems to mind, and I can't bring myself to care. Especially when I spot Linc walking toward me. I smile again at his loosened tie. When I stalker spied on him during the party, he kept tugging on the silky dark material that matched his eyes. If he hates ties so much, he didn't have to wear one. None of the Bishops would have minded. There's something incredibly sexy about a man in a suit sans tie. I privately applauded my father's recent decision for ties to be optional when dressing for the games and travel.

Linc reaches the table, and I scoot over to give him more space on the bench. "Thanks," he gives a nod. "Hey, Quakes." Linc studies his teammates. "Beers and pizzas are on their way."

A collective cheer sounds from the cluster of four tables. Several players stand and head over to an open cornhole board, while others opt for darts. Leaving only a few of us behind as we wait for the food and drinks.

"Sorry again for my asshole behavior, both in the car and at the party." Linc's voice is pitched low, so only I can hear it. "I've been in a funk. I can't seem to shake." He runs a hand through the longer top layers of his hair, messing the black strands into the perfect disarray of just-had-sex bedhead. Double sigh.

"Is it your play?" I murmur to match our private conversation.

He frowns. "Yeah, some." His hands fist. "I feel like I'm letting the team down. Letting the fans down."

I wish I could give him words of comfort, but there's a reason I want to trade him. It makes me uncomfortable to see how depressed he is. I stare past his shoulder, not wanting to keep eye contact, so it's easy to spot the man guiding a little boy who could be no more than five or six our way.

This makes me smile, and I tap Linc's shoulder and gesture for him to turn around. The father and son stop a few feet away when the dad gives the boy a little push.

"Go on, it'll be fine."

The little boy glances at his father before shyly approaching Linc, who slides off the bench, crouching, making himself as kid-level as possible for a man his size.

"Hey," Linc offers his fist to bump, and the boy's wide eyes grow larger.

"Hi," the kid bumps his tiny fist against Linc's.

"I'm Lincoln—"

"I know," the boy interrupts, bouncing on his feet in excitement.

Linc grins. "What's your name?"

"I'm Pete. You're number thirty-three, Lincoln Cavanaugh. You won two Cups!" This makes Linc laugh.

"Do you play hockey, Pete?" The boy nods his head up and down like a demented bobblehead doll. "What's your position?"

"I'm a goalie, just like you!"

"You are? That's awesome, buddy."

"I want to be just like you. I'm gonna play for the NHL and win Cups."

"I don't doubt it. Where do you practice?"

"Um," he shoots a glance at his father, who approaches, hand out.

Linc shakes hands, still in his crouch. I would have thought his old injuries would bother him, but he's at ease, as if he could hang that way for hours. They may be aging, but his legs are still strong from the years of repetition in goal.

"He's in the Little Tremblers program at the Burbank rink."

"I know it well. No practice until the New Year, right?"

"That's correct," the kid's father confirms.

"Pete, you want a photo with me?"

The little boy's eyes grow round again, and nods enthusiastically. The dad pulls out his phone as Linc pulls Pete in close and smiles at the camera.

I stand and smile. "Would you like a photo with Linc? I'm happy to take one for you."

"Thanks, I'm Rob." I take his phone, and he picks up Pete, holding him on his hip. Linc stands. "I appreciate this. Pete's a huge fan. We both are."

"My pleasure."

They all smile as I shoot a bunch of photos, and then I hand the phone back to Rob.

"So, would you like tickets to the next home game?" I offer. This time, it's Rob's eyes growing large.

"Sure, that would be amazing."

"Let me get your contact information, and I'll have them at will call." I spot his wedding ring. "How many? Perhaps your wife or other children?"

"Two more kids and my wife would kill me if she couldn't go."

"Five it is. Not a problem."

Smiles all around as they depart. Linc is transformed after his interaction with his tiny hero-worshiping fan. He's grinning, his dimple is out, and his eyes have a sparkle that's been missing for a while. I'm transfixed. The man is gorgeous, and he stops my heart. I'll miss him when he's gone. When I force him to leave.

The beer and food arrive, and like locusts swarming, so do the players and their plus ones.

Luka pitches a pepperoni across the table, and the meat smacks Linc in the face. "Dude," he calls out. It's funny hearing such California slang with a Slovenian accent. "Who's the tiny tot?" The players all wear matching grins as if they are all in on some private joke.

Linc pops the thrown pepperoni in his mouth and chews before grinning, releasing his dimple out into the wild again. Gah! "Pete's a goalie from the Little Tremblers out of Burbank."

"Let us know when you're going." Zach throws out.

"Yeah," Brian agrees. "I want in, too."

Going? My confusion must be apparent because Zach takes pity and explains.

"Our man, Cavie, has a secret superpower. Little hockey players all over town are drawn to him."

"That's because they know he'll show at practices and skate with them," Luka informs.

"He does?" I glance at Linc and see his cheeks are pink. "How did I not know this? This is marketing gold—"

"Nope, no cameras. This is something just for me and the kids." Linc shakes his head. "When it's a team thing, fine, but not when I'm on my own."

I sit a bit stunned. "Okay, sure, but at least let me gather some signed jerseys and sticks for the little guys—"

"And gals," Zach throws in. "It's not necessary. Linc has it handled. And no ditching us like last time. It'll be the four amigos, or I will hunt you down."

The whole table teases and trash-talks Linc, all in good fun, but I see he's getting uncomfortable. Apparently, Linc didn't want his visits to the kids made public. Or at least to me. It's time to rescue him. I racked my brain for a topic changer when it hits me because I always wanted to know the answer.

"Hey, can I ask you a question?" His shoulders tense, no doubt in anticipation I'll ask about his secret hobby. "Why do you always have Stewie from *The Family Guy* somewhere on your helmet?"

The table laughs, and Linc visibly relaxes. "I started skating at two, at least according to my parents. When I was four, they entered me into the hockey system. The game came naturally after that. My parents didn't have a lot of money, but somehow, they managed and supported me. I was a late bloomer and didn't start my growth spurt until I was sixteen." His smile turns to chagrin. "I moved up to play in the 14U, and suddenly everyone was bigger, stronger, faster, and I was no longer one of the best players on the team."

Zach laughs. "It happens to all of us, Cavie."

"True, but my thirteen-year-old brain took a huge confidence hit." He shrugs. "My sister Patty noticed and did something that changed everything."

"What was that?" I remember he's from a large family, with Linc being the oldest of a brood of seven. Most likely, he was the sibling protector and anchor, and it must have been special for someone to look out for him for a change.

"I was sitting in the backyard in a funk as only a hormonal teenager can be when she marched over and dropped a stuffed Stewie onto my lap." He smiles at the fond memory. "Patty proceeded to tell me, 'Stewie is small but the master of his universe and will someday take over the world.' She said, 'Be like Stewie,' but instead of the world, I should take over hockey." He chuckles. "Stewie lived in my game bag as a reminder. When I earned enough money and had my first personalized mask, Stewie had to be on it. Sometimes, it's sneaky, and you have to search for him. Other times, he's out in the open. Now he's always with me on game day."

Oh, man. All the feels right now. "That's pretty cool, Linc." I give him a smile before grabbing my beer to hide behind. This man. He's so getting to me. Seeing him with his tiny mini-me, knowing he goes out of his way to mentor with no publicity, secretly giving his time to kids. Yikes, I'm in danger. I'm starting to have feelings for him. Which I can't do. It's fine to have a secret crush on this sexy, gorgeous man, but that's simple lust. How can I trade him if I'm falling for him?

CHAPTER Five

LINCOLN

"That workout was intense." Luka rubs a towel over his face, removing the dripping sweat from his hair and head.

A thousand agreements rush through my mind. I feel great. Not a twinge in my hip. In fact, there hasn't been any significant pain since getting physical with Holt at the Bishops' holiday party. Today, I could do an actual split, which I haven't done since the start of the season. There's something appealing about beating on Holt more often if it means increased flexibility.

"I told you so, you mother-f-ers." Brian crows as he pulls ingredients from his fridge and places them on the counter.

Zach, Luka, and I gather round the large island in Bri's kitchen, nodding in agreement. I make myself useful and grab the blender while Zach and Luka fight over a butcher knife.

"Guys, knock it off. One of you'll hurt yourselves, and then where will we be? Out of the fucking playoffs." Brian grabs the knife away from them and turns to the fruits and veggies piled in front of him. As he chops, I take the pieces and toss them into the blender. Zach grabs the protein whey and dumps some in.

We always drink a superfood shake after a workout if we can. The protein, fiber, Omega-3, vitamins, and minerals are good for muscle recovery. Once everything is blended and poured, we stand around the island and drink. After a few sips, Ribi breaks the silence.

"So, I couldn't help but notice how chummy you are with Catherine." He smirks. "Is there something you want to share with the class?"

"Don't start." I grab the back of my neck, hoping to hold off a blush. *Dammit*.

"Oh my God, there is!" Brian points a finger at me. "You grab your neck when uncomfortable."

"Can't blame you, man," Luka nods. "She's hot."

"And our boss," Zach adds.

How is this my life? "There's nothing going on. She's not into me that way."

"But you want her to be, right?"

Shit. Fuck. Damn. Are Slovenians freaking mind readers?

The truth is, I am attracted to her, but it scares me. I don't have the best track record as far as romance goes. While Catherine was off earning her business degrees, I managed to get entangled with a puck bunny, one of the single women who hang out at the rink or MacKay's and live to seduce professional hockey players. Everyone—my teammates, my mom, and even the coach—warned me that getting involved with Rainbow was a bad idea. And yes, that was her actual name on her driver's license, Rainbow Raine. Of course, being a young moron, I didn't listen, and after knowing her for a grand total of six months, we went to Vegas to celebrate the team winning the Cup and somehow wound up getting married. And when I say somehow, I mean there was a lot of alcohol involved. I can't wait until it happens to Holt. Man, I'll laugh my ass off.

To be fair, things with Rain were pretty good for a while. We got married at the end of the season and spent the summer fucking. My house, the condo in Maui, the airplane on the way home from Hawaii. You name it, we fucked there. I wouldn't level up what we did by calling it making love because, in hindsight, that was the only part of each other's anatomy we never came close to touching—our hearts.

Then the season started, and for a hockey fan, Rain was surprised at the amount of time I spent on the road with the team. I mean, she had to know how away games worked, right? We didn't even get to the end of the season before she left me for an AHL player. I never found out how she handled their travel schedule and didn't care.

I realized when she left, I wasn't really in love with her either, but her leaving hurt all the same. Not because it broke my heart, but it definitely shattered any belief I had that a hockey marriage could work. I don't know how Sonny and Jenny do it or any of the other married guys, but I'm not willing to try it again, at least not until road trips are no longer an issue. Which, dammit, could be looming in my all too near future.

I'm so lost in my own thoughts I nearly miss it when Brian says, "Did you guys hear about Simpson on the Warriors? They put him on waivers, and nobody picked him up." There are murmurs of sympathy all around the kitchen, but I'm screaming *shit* in my head. The dude is three years younger than me and a forward. He'd been having a rough couple of seasons, plagued by what the league euphemistically calls a "lower-body injury," but in a forward, that could mean anything from a muscle pull to a shattered kneecap. They keep it quiet on purpose, so assholes like Holt don't take advantage of a weakness, but if he kept re-injuring whatever it was, that makes coming back all that much more difficult.

I'd be a terrible poker player, and my thoughts are plastered all over my face. Zach puts a hand on my shoulder and shakes me. "That's not you, man. You're not going anywhere. Coach and the Bishops, *all* the Bishops, wouldn't allow it. You know what Coach says, a player's worth is more than just his stats."

Maybe. And maybe that was reason enough to stay away from Catherine. If she is on the verge of taking over, there's no need to make her job any more difficult by getting involved with a player whose whole life she'll be forced to destroy for the good of the team.

X

I smile as I pull open the door to the L.A. Quakes Ice at the Pickwick Gardens in Burbank, where the Little Tremblers are getting ready to practice. Only their coaches know we're planning to attend. That's right, Bri, Ribi, and Sonny follow behind me. We're all carrying two gear bags. One with our own stuff, and the other filled with freebies for the kids—autographed photos, signed jerseys, signed sticks, and pucks. Marla, in marketing, is the only one who knows what I do in my spare time. One call, and she wrangles all the stuff when I have a head count and date. She even puts in extras in case parents or coaches want memorabilia.

My favorite part? When I skate onto the ice for the first time and the kids notice. Some are stunned, but there is always grinning. It's no different this time, especially since I'm bringing the Quakes' captain, one of the hottest leftwingers in the league, and Brian, who's our lead scorer this season. Since this is a surprise, my friends and I put on our skates in the lobby, so it's a simple matter of dropping our bags on the bench, peeling off our blade guards, and hopping the boards.

Pete spots us first. "Lincoln! You came!" Forgetting about

practice, the little guy skates toward me, gaining respectable speed. I brace for impact as his sturdy body collides with mine, wrapping my legs in a hug.

"Hey, Pete." I pat his helmet. He stares at me with stars in his eyes.

"You brought more teammates!"

"I sure did." I take his tiny gloved hand in my large one and start skating to where the Tremblers are standing in lines in front of the coaches. My friends are right behind me when we stop next to the staff, and I give the boy a gentle push. "Go get back in formation."

Coach Greer holds out a hand, which I shake. "Thanks for doing this, it means the world to the kids."

"It's our pleasure." My teammates nod along in agreement.

Greer introduces us to the tiny players, and as I gaze over the group, I'm happy to see a lot of girls. This isn't always the case at this age, so I'm glad their numbers are growing. Usually, they'd rather be figure skating. We're about to break into groups for drills when I hear another pair of skates hit the ice. Turning, I'm stunned to see Catherine gliding toward us.

I spin and whisper-shout, "Who the hell invited her?" while glaring at my friends.

"Um," Ribi raises a hand. "I thought since she was interested, she could tag along."

My lips thin into a frown. All three of them bust out laughing. Oh shit, this is a setup.

"Hey. Sorry, I'm late. Traffic coming over the hill was murder." She murmurs to us, then smiles and gives a wave at the kids. "Hi everyone, I think I missed the intros. I'm Catherine Bishop. My father, Robert Bishop, is the owner of the Los Angeles Quakes. I'm not the best hockey player, so I hope you'll teach me."

Which is bullshit. I know she played in college. They

weren't champs or anything, but she knows her way around the ice. I smile, knowing she's fibbing for the kids' sake.

And she's adorable. She threaded her ponytail through the back of her Quakes' baseball cap. Her hair swishes back and forth every time she moves. She must have gotten the memo because she's dressed identically to us, from hockey skates, black snow pants, and a Quakes' sweater, though hers isn't numbered. It's a blank. The hockey gloves swallow her hands, but she holds her stick like she knows how to use it.

Since the introductions are finished, the kids break into groups for drills, and my teammates spread out to help. The time flies, and my cheeks hurt from the constant smiling.

Then Sonny yells over in that commanding captain's voice, "Caveman, little help in the right circle." I snap to it, instinctively following his orders because, on the ice, he's the leader. We all follow and would do anything for him. Then I realize he's sending me over to Catherine, who is having trouble teaching a little girl how to skate backward. Ribi and Bri are both closer, so his master plan isn't exactly subtle. If there weren't kids around, I'd tell him where to shove it, but we're here for them, so I skate over to help.

"There seems to be a bit of a balance problem over here."

"I'm a good skater," Catherine states. "But apparently not the best instructor."

"No worries," I crouch in front of the little skater. "What's your name?"

"Lacey."

"Nice to meet you, Lacey. Can I show you something?"

She nods her head frantically, and my smile turns into a grin. I stand and hold my stick across my body and lower it to her height. "Grab on with both hands." She does. Next, I bend my knees a little and lean a tiny bit forward at my waist. "Okay, copy me." Lacey does, and I start skating forward. She's pushed along with her grip on my stick. "Good. Keep moving your skates. Excellent. Now take one hand off." Her balance wobbles, but she recovers. "Great job. Now, without losing your position, I want you to let go and keep skating."

She looks a little nervous but follows through. She remains upright and skates backward. "Awesome, Lacey. Look at you go."

"I'm doing it! I've got this." Her voice filled with pride and smiles.

"Yes, you do. Keep going." I encourage her and step to the side, watching her skate away.

Catherine skates over. "You're pretty amazing yourself. It's like you have this magical touch. I spent almost twenty minutes with Lacey and got nowhere. You skate by, and in less than a minute, she can skate backward on her own."

Before I can reply, I'm slammed from behind, cut off at the knees. I fall forward into Catherine, and we both go down. A little boy does a victory circle around us before skating off. I hear my friends laughing, those fuckers. I've got to be crushing her, so I move my weight to my arms and look down. "Are you all right? Did you hit your head?" We aren't wearing helmets. I don't want her to move if she's hurt. It's when I'm staring at her that I realize how incredible she feels beneath me, all soft and curvy. I need to banish those thoughts before my cock gets ideas. There's no way she wouldn't notice in this position.

"I think I'm good."

"Okay, let's take it slow." I get to my feet and hold out a hand, pulling her up. She's standing close, so it's easy to touch the back of her head. "Any pain or tenderness?"

"N-no, I-I'm fine."

I stare into her eyes. They're an amazing combination of brown and green. This woman. There's so much more to her than anyone knows. Screw it. I'm going for it.

"Catherine," I whisper.

"Y-yes?"

I lean a little closer, our noses almost touching. "Have

dinner with me? Sunday." This close, I can see her eyes dilate with my question. She's attracted to me. "Come on, say yes."

"It's a bad idea," she whispers back.

"Probably, but let's do it anyway," I smirk because I can't help myself.

"Okay."

"Okay." I smile and skate backward, away from her. This is either the best decision ever or the worst mistake of my life.

CHAPTER Six

CATHERINE

I'm about to order another iced tea when Brittany breezes into the crowded downtown restaurant, her usual twenty minutes late. I love Brit. We suffered the slings and arrows of the male-dominated MBA program together, but one of these days, I'm going to realize I need to tell her we're meeting half an hour earlier than we are so she'll be on time. Of course, she's shrewd as hell. She'd figure it out and adapt.

After ordering iced tea for me and a vodka martini for her, as well as our salads, she leans in, eyes gleaming. "So, I saw the Instagram reel of you and the hunky hockey god cuddling on the ice. Do tell?"

I hang my head and groan. Some parent captured a video of the little Trembler racing toward Linc from behind, taking him out and me with him. Our marketing team spotted it and posted it on the Quakes' social media feeds. It's gone kind of viral, with comments of the kid being the next great blueliner. It's pretty cute, but I know publicity is the last thing Lincoln wanted.

"It's nothing."

"So you two aren't knocking boots, or I guess, in this case, skates?" She sucks the olive off the martini stirrer in a way that has all the businessmen sitting at the three closest tables stammering and making sure their napkins cover their entire laps. Brit laughs. She's always been able to manipulate men while I stood in her shadow, unnoticed, the whole time we were in school together. It might have bugged me if I weren't so focused on learning.

"No, don't be ridiculous. I mean, he asked me out, but I think I'm going to cancel."

Thank goodness she'd swallowed her sip of her drink, or I would have ended up wearing it. "What? Why? You're insane. Here, let me remind you of what you'd be missing." With a quick couple of flicks of her fingers, she opened the Quakes' Instagram account. A few days ago, they'd posted a picture of Linc and Brian shirtless at the beach, throwing a football.

"I didn't even think you liked hockey. Why are you following the team?" I'm stunned. Also, drinking in the sight of Linc. Brian is good-looking, no doubt, but Linc is chiseled like a god, with thighs that could hold me in any position. *OMG, am I getting damp just thinking about it?* I tear my gaze away to look at my salad.

"*Pfft*, sporty sweaty stuff isn't my thing. However, since my bestie is about to become the owner, now I have to pay attention. So why in the name of all that's sexy would you cancel your date?"

"Brit, the guy is my employee. If the situation were reversed, if I went out on a date with my boss, everyone would assume he was coercing me. Or I'm trying to sleep my way to the top. It's not illegal, but it's definitely frowned upon."

My friend grimaces. "In your case, it would be both since your boss is your dad, and eww."

Despite my mood, that makes me laugh. "You know what I mean."

"Yes, I actually do, but there's something else going on. I can tell from that guilty look on your face." She leaned in closer and whispered, "Come on, spill it."

How can she read me like a book, and yet I'm never sure what's going to come out of her mouth next? I lean in to meet her, desperate to keep this confidential. "You know how hockey has a certain time when you trade players?"

With a glare, she comments, "I don't know a puck from a duck, but yes, I'm aware that sporty teams trade…oh!" Realization dawns on her face, and her eyes dance in amusement.

"Yeah, oh," I repeat with a lot less glee. "I don't want to, but it's better for the team if we put him on waivers or trade him and make room for a new—"

"Younger," she interrupts with a shake of her head. "Well, I guess it's nice once in a while to see it happen to a man."

Only it isn't. It isn't nice at all for any athlete, but especially not for one I'm developing feelings for.

"Still don't see the problem," she said in between mouthfuls of salad. "Why not scratch your itch and fuck him out of your system? There's no conflict because he'll be gone by March or earlier."

Off the team, out of my life, but I'm not sure there's enough fucking in the world to get him out of my system.

It feels weird getting ready for a date on a Sunday late afternoon, but such is life in hockey. The Quakes had a game yesterday, and most players try to keep the curfew the night before, hence the regular Friday or Saturday date night was off the table. I put my lip gloss down and study my reflection in the mirror. Good to go. I leave the bathroom and enter my bedroom. Linc said casual and comfortable, so I'm dressed in jeans and a long-sleeved green Henley. My slip-on flats are by the front door, and I grab a hoodie from the closet. January in Southern California is tricky. The weather is spectacular today, but it might get chilly later.

My doorbell sounds, and my stomach clenches. Right on time. I almost canceled this date about twenty times this week but somehow never went through with it. Honestly, I'm curious about where Linc is taking me. Most men I go out with find the trendiest, fanciest restaurant trying to impress me. This can't be the case with Linc, since no high-end catery would seat me dressed as I am.

I slip my feet into the flats, grab my purse, and open the door. He stands there with his hands in his jeans pockets and a plain blue T-shirt, which makes his normal steel-gray eyes appear bluish.

"Hey," he greets me and throws a chin nod my way.

"Hi." I step outside, lock my door, and turn to him. Without a word, he steps next to me and places a hand on the small of my back, guiding me to his Corvette. Like a gentleman, he opens the passenger door for me and then closes it. I study him as he crosses in front of the hood, taking the opportunity to check out his ass in those jeans. Yummy.

He gets in, starts the car, and shoots me a glance before backing out of my driveway. What was that look? Linc can't be nervous, can he? He's always been so confident around me. Or am I getting the freaking silent treatment again like I did on the drive to MacKay's the night of the party? All he's spoken so far was a, *hey*. I shoot my own glance his way, catching his tight hold on the steering wheel. Something isn't right, but I'll be damned if I'll ask him. He was the one who wanted a date. If this keeps up, I'll ride-share app myself home wherever we end up.

I keep my sigh internal, hoping we get there soon. This is

bullshit. My anger builds with each silent mile that goes by. Echo Park Lake? I realize that must be our destination when he circles the park, his eyes scanning for a parking spot. Finding a space on the street is never easy in L.A., but with the ton of food vans stationed around the perimeter, spots are scarcer than ever.

He's taking me to dinner at a food truck? The thought almost makes me smile and forget I'm pissed at him. Linc slides into a space with the precision of a surgeon and parks. Still no words. I get out when he does and wait for him on the lake side of the car. When he reaches me, he guides me toward the trucks in complete silence. Enough. When we reach the lawn, I halt and spin to confront him.

"What the hell, Cavanaugh? It was your idea to go on this date. If I wanted to spend time with a sullen asshole, I'd go out with Holt."

He pushes a hand through his hair. "This is a mistake."

"Obviously. Why the hell didn't you cancel?" My voice rises with my anger. "Why the charade of picking me up and taking me here?"

"I thought I'd get over it." His own voice grows louder as he argues back.

"Over what?" This is ridiculous. I can't believe I'm standing here arguing with Lincoln Cavanaugh. I should have never opened the door. But he's kind of hot with his scowl and sparking gaze.

"You posted the video all over the Quakes' feeds." He barks. "The one thing,"—he holds a single finger in the air—"I asked you was no publicity, no cameras."

"What? You, moron. I did no such thing!" As I realize what this is all about, I'm flummoxed. Does he not understand how social media works? "I didn't have you filmed. If you recall, I was on the ice when you wiped out. Did you see a camera crew?" I blow out a frustrated breath, though I am impressed he's willing to go toe-to-toe. Most men are intimidated by me. Well, except for my dad, brothers, and, of course, the GM. "You've been mad at me all week for nothing. Why the hell didn't you come to me earlier instead of stewing like a sullen teenager?"

"I was angry. And it's not nothing. I wanted privacy."

"Then I guess your friends shouldn't have invited me." I throw my hands into the air with disgust. "You know what? I'm going to give you all the privacy you want. I'm out of here." Marching off, I get two strides before his grip on my arm halts me.

"Catherine."

Oh no, he doesn't. One glance at his hand, and he drops his hold. "I'm done. You're a professional athlete. You know how social media works. Some dad or mom filmed their kid and hashtagged the shit out of it, and the marketing department"—I shake my head—"not me, spotted it and reposted." I glare at him. "At least there's one thing we can agree on, this was definitely a mis—"

I'm cut off mid-rant by the simple method of Linc's lips crashing into mine in a ravishing kiss. Stunned, I gasp, and he doesn't hesitate as he slides his tongue inside, tasting me. I burst into flames. He moves his hands. One wraps around the back of my neck, holding me in place, and the other curls around my waist, tugging me flush against him. Oh God, he's hard all over. My arms wrap around his neck, and my fingers dive into his hair, holding on, trying to get closer. He tastes so good, minty fresh, and all male. A groan slips out. This man can kiss. I rub against his obvious arousal, and it's his turn to moan.

He slows down, retreats, and peppers my lips with softer kisses. When he reaches the corner of my mouth, he pulls away to press his forehead against mine.

"I'm sorry," he whispers. "You're right, I'm a fucking idiot."

"You are. I can't believe you thought I'd betray you." I'm kind of hurt. I pride myself on my promises and my honor.

His arms wrap around me and squeeze. "I'm sorry." He huffs out a breath that caresses my skin. "The kid thing is something I do for myself, and I just...I don't know. Please forgive me."

"Okay," I hug him back before straightening and stepping out of his hold. "But this is strike two."

His hand rubs the back of his neck. "Thanks, I get it. No more fucking things up." Linc gives me a sad smile. "Thanks for giving me a second chance." He gestures toward the food trucks. "Can I show you my favorite guilty pleasure? You don't have to eat from the van. There're plenty of others to choose from, so don't feel obligated."

He takes my hand, intertwining our fingers, and starts walking.

"So, what's the truck called?"

"Ricky's Fish Tacos. The best ever." He grins at me. "Word on the street is he catches all the fish and shrimp himself, so the food is super fresh. It's a secret where his fishing hole is." He squeezes our joined hands and grins. "His truck is normally near a beach, so I'm glad I checked." With his free hand, he gestures to the park. "I guess this is some special event."

"Well, lucky me, and this sounds delicious." We reach Ricky's truck and get in line. The food smells amazing from back here. "I could eat fish tacos."

"Really? You won't regret it. You'll love 'em."

"I'm surprised you'd eat food truck fare during the season. Nutritional guidelines, eating healthy, and all that."

He chuckles. "I burn a lot of calories on the ice. A guilty pleasure once in a while won't do any damage." He slaps his abs.

Um, yeah, if he's been gorging on fried fish tacos, it doesn't show. He's solid muscle, which now I'm intimately familiar with after being pressed against him. And wow, that kiss. I wouldn't mind doing that again. We order and find a place to sit. It doesn't take long for our number to be announced. Linc gestures for me to stay put, and he jumps from the ground to standing, mind you, without using either his hands or arms. He returns and sits as gracefully, handing me my tacos. The scent alone tells me these are going to be winners.

I take a bite, chew, and groan. He grins.

"I told you. The. Best. Ever."

I nod and take another bite. We chat over tacos and beers. Insignificant stuff, getting to know you kind of things. This date may have started rocky, but it's turned enchanting. Street tacos in a park. How in the world did he figure me out? That *this* is the type of date I would always prefer. Fancy, trendy restaurants have their place, but having to be in business mode most of the time, it's nice to just relax. He has the money to go all out, yet he chooses perfectly.

This man. So many wonderful hidden traits I'm discovering. I'll have to watch myself. The more I glimpse into the heart of Lincoln Cavanaugh, the more he slips into my thoughts. Brit told me to lust and fuck, but that might not be an option anymore.

CHAPTER Seven

LINCOLN

I brace my weight on my hockey stick as I watch Patrik Eklund, our young rookie from Sweden, skating away, along with two of our AHL players from the Ontario Tsunami.

"Okay, Eeks. You've got this. Remember your edges. Channel your inner Sonny, and keep skating." I don't use a whistle like our coaches, so I shout, "Go."

Eeks tears down center ice with the puck as the other guys give chase. Patrik crosses the blue line and enters the offensive zone, head up and skating his breakaway. The boys catch him at the same time, making an Eeks sandwich. But the Swede has momentum and skill, keeping his edges so he powers through. With a loud *thwack*, the puck goes sailing into the empty net. The kid throws his hands in the air in a victory celly.

"Great job, Eeks. Your edges were perfect. Sonny better watch himself. You'll be gunning for his position on the first line if he isn't careful."

Patrik glides over with the biggest grin. "I think I finally understand. That time, there was no way I was going down. For a goalie, you sure can skate."

I chuckle because I started skating as a two-year-old, or at least my parents have photographic proof. After all, I was too young to remember. Also, I wasn't always a goalie. When I was a tiny tot, I skated defense from age four to eight. When our team's goalie got the flu, and we had no backup, Coach asked for a volunteer. No one wanted to, and I didn't want the team to default, so I raised my hand. The rest is history. I loved being in the crease and never wanted to leave. Still don't. But there is one drawback to being a goalie—skating. I love flying down the ice and handling the puck, so I haven't given it up. I skate and play with a biscuit every chance I get. Mostly, it's during the off season, but I also make opportunities during our busy schedule, or times like these when I'm helping the rookies or our youth hockey program.

"Thanks, Eeks. I'm glad I could help." It's a mystery to me why the rookies and young players come to me for pointers. Being a goalie, I'm not the most obvious coach for a forward or D-man. But what the hell, I love to skate and watch young talent grow.

I grab the bucket of pucks and toss the contents into the neutral zone, where they scatter. "Okay, rookies, shooting drill. I want to see top shelf, tip-ins, and sneaky five-holes, well, if we had a goalie."

"You're here, Caveman," Ecks replies. "You should suit up."

I clap the kid on the shoulder. "With my long, thick goalie blades? Then I couldn't show you the edge work. Now get out there and start passing and shooting."

The young men skate to the other blue line, laughing and chirping each other. The Quakes and Tsunami talent pool was pretty amazing, with a bunch of gifted up-and-comers. There will be a Stanley Cup in their future.

Tomlin is skating with his head down again, so I zip in and steal the puck, then pass to Eeks, who tips it into the net.

"Why'd you lose the puck, Mark?"

He looks down and then faces me. "My head wasn't up, and I didn't see you coming."

"Right answer. Go again."

They reset and start. This time, Mark Tomlin's eyes are focused, his head on a swivel. He's left wing on the triangle formation, his fast pass to Ansel Ricar's stick smacks the tape on the center blueline, and with only a split second of pause, he passes to Eeks, who's on right wing at the dot. The moment the puck hits his stick, he pulls back and makes a glorious slapshot for a top-shelf goal. The perfect tic-tack-toe. It looks like my job here is done.

"Okay, guys, gather the pucks and put the net away. It can't get any better than that. Outstanding work today."

The men shout their thanks, and with no complaints, they clean the ice. That's when I notice Jason Toll standing in the exit, ankles and arms crossed as he leans on the frame. He gives me a chin nod, and I skate over. Tall and fit, the man's a veteran Quake who I skated with on our first Stanley Cup winning team. He retired that season, saying he reached his goals and it was time to move on. I wish I knew how he did that. It wasn't like he was ancient or anything. He was two years younger than I am right now and still had plenty of play left in him.

I stop in front of him and cross my arms against my chest. "Spying on me, Tolli?"

He chuckles and straightens. "It's not the first time. I just let you see me this time."

"Creeper much?"

"It's when I do my best scouting. Got a minute to chat?"

"Sure. The kids are probably out of the locker room. You can talk while I change."

"Sounds good."

He follows me through the hallway and into the locker room. I plop down on a seat and raise an eyebrow, wondering what in the hell Jason Tolls wants. He smiles, and I start unlacing my skates.

"You're really good with the rookies."

"Thanks, man."

"And the little tykes. You can't hide that shit. It gets around. You're such a natural at mentoring and keeping the grassroots growing."

I nod, a little embarrassed by the praise, as heat flushes my neck, reaching my face. "Yeah, Eeks asked for some advice, I was happy to help." I duck back down, pretending I need eyes on my laces to remove my skates. Jason Tolls is a legend, and apparently, he's been stalking me.

"And I'm sure the others jumped at the chance to work with you and Patrik, right?"

"Um, something like that."

"Have you thought about what you want to do when you retire?"

Deciding to face the music, I sit up and shrug. "Not really. I'm not ready to give up the game. It's all I know. I just want to play."

Jason sits next to me. "Been there, done that."

"I don't get it. You were on top of your game. Got the Cup and gave it all away."

He smiles. "I never gave anything away."

I shake my head. He had two more seasons in him, at the very least, and could have added another Stanley Cup to his name.

"I see what you're thinking," he paused. "Keep in mind, I already had a Cup win when I skated with the Toronto Ice. I've won both the Conn Smythe and Hart Memorial trophies, plus the Mark Messier Leadership award, twice, and an Olympic medal." Jason smiles. "I'd reached all my goals and preferred to go out on top instead of an injury ending my career. Besides. I missed a lot of my kids growing up by chasing my dreams. And my wife was certainly owed a break. It was the easiest call I ever made."

I shake my head. He really had accomplished it all. So much so, losing out on another Cup didn't even faze him. I'm sure getting inducted into the Hall Of Fame didn't hurt his retirement decision, either. Could be I waited too long and should have gone out after the second championship. Doubt creeps in, but it's too late to turn back the clock. What's done is done.

"What about working for the team? You're a legend here, Linc. This organization would give you any spot of your choice. You know that, right?"

I stare at Tolli, not feeling like a legend, more like a loser. "Are you here because I suck and the team wants to clear cap space?"

My question elicits an outright laugh from Jason. "No, just no," he replies after he gets himself under control. He smacks a hand on the back of my head. "You don't suck. Get out of your head. Every player in the league goes through a down period. It won't get better if you start labeling yourself. So just stop, all right?"

"Yeah, yeah." I grip the back of my neck. "It's just…maybe I've stayed in the game too long. Should have taken your path, but I don't have the family motivation you had. Playing hockey is all I know."

"You're wrong, man. I've been watching you."

"You do know how that sounds, Tolli, right?"

He chuckles. "You learn a lot about a person if they don't realize they're being observed. I found as a part of player development it's given me a sharp edge. And you, Caveman, you might think all you have is being a goalie, but that's not even remotely true."

"So, are you gonna tell me or skate around all day?"

"Okay, blunt it is. I want you on my team. You'd be

awesome for player development. Fuck, man, you're already doing the job, just not getting paid for it. All the mentoring and teaching? You're the perfect fit, with proven skills. Who knew under all the goalie gear isn't only an amazing skater, but an instructor as well?"

Stunned, I stare at him, dazed. My pulse races. He wants me to work with him? And he tells me I'm already doing it? I never imagined working for the team other than as a goalie.

"I can see I've thrown you for a loop." Jason stands. "Think about it. Please give it serious consideration." He heads for the exit. "And get out of your head and start winning us games again. You're a beast, so channel it. You got this."

With those parting words, he disappears. Sitting on the bench, a smile turns into a grin. I realized there's another plus to hanging up my player skates. The weird discomfort of a player dating the owner would disappear if I retire. There's no perceived conflict if I work in development. I've been attracted to Catherine for what feels like forever. And now that I've kissed her? It feels special, like something could grow between us if given the time and opportunity. I've watched the married guys on the team and never understood how they managed time for a family. If I stop playing, could I have what they've got?

X

"Come on guys, the Albion is supposed to be awesome," Trevor, our third-line D-man and the team's playboy, cajoles. "The rooftop bar is the newest hotspot to pick up women."

Two days later, we're back in the locker room, showered and changing after a hard-fought win against the Tampa Bay Flash. I, of course, rode the bench. The boys played an electric back-forth wild game, constantly falling behind and then tying up. It was Bri's goal in the last thirty seconds in the third that gave us the win in regulation, in a game everyone thought we'd lose. Needless to say, the locker room is pumped, and the music is blaring.

"I'm game," Sean throws in.

Like the first rock in an avalanche, most of the young players jump in. This is looking like a recipe for disaster. We've got an early flight to catch for our East Coast road games. The gang of young and dumb hustles out as I shake my head.

"Cave, Bri," Zach calls out.

We both glance over, all too aware of what's coming.

"I hate to ask, but I need you to go to the Albion and keep an eye on them."

"Shit, man, really?" Brian runs a hand through his damp hair.

"I'd go, but I promised Jenny I'd be home. We're gonna be gone for ten days. Please, do the team a solid."

I sigh and exchange a look with Bri. Of course, Zach wants to spend time with his wife, and sometimes, being single has its downsides. "Sure, Sonny."

"Thanks, guys. It means the world. Please keep them out of trouble so they can get on the plane tomorrow."

"They're all adults," Brian declares. "Can't stop the stupid if they're determined."

"True, but they look up to both of you. You can probably prevent most of them from their idiocy. And Trevor, he'll be fine. Our manwhore knows how to take care of himself."

This makes me laugh. Too true. I guess I'll be going to the rooftop bar at the Albion.

CHAPTER
Eight

CATHERINE

I am so bored right now it's all I can do not to have my head bob as I nod off. The sleazeball coefficient is the only thing keeping Todd Johnson from putting me to sleep altogether. Every time I point out another positive about doing business with Bishop Tech, he leers at me with this oily smile. The meeting isn't about the team, but I keep my hands active in all the family businesses so I can hold a conversation about any of them.

From the way this guy is looking at me, it's clear he thinks I'm dessert and not an actual human being. What did Daniel tell him? Asshat to both of them. The only thing keeping me engaged is thinking of all the creative ways to kill my brother for setting this parlay. He was supposed to deal with Mr. Sleazeball but had to bow out at the last minute and begged me to take it. Things have been tense between us ever since Dad made it official. He'd be handing the Quakes over to me when it came time, so I agreed to do this favor in an attempt to mend fences, even though I did nothing wrong. Next time, I'll send him flowers or candy instead.

My first clue that something was *hinky,* as our father likes to say, was his choice of venue. Usually, when I meet a business associate for dinner in downtown L.A., I opt for The Palm or Mastro's. So when he suggested Albion's rooftop bar, the little voice in the back of my head warned me something was off. But just because you have an MBA doesn't mean you always make smart choices. For Daniel's sake, I agreed, not wanting to seem argumentative.

I'm the only person in the place wearing a suit, including El Creepo. We order dinner, the drinks arrive first, and somewhere before the server brings the salads, his hand lands on my knee. I grit my teeth and remove the offending appendage while carrying on extolling the virtues of doing business with us.

I've barely touched my wine, but he's on to his third Old Fashioned. Touching my knee graduates to stroking my thigh, and the third time I have to remove his hand, I might have bent his pinky backward. From the way he's howling, you'd think I'd gone all She-Hulk on him and torn it off.

"You bitch," he hisses, a little spittle on his lower lip.

That's my cue to exit. Someone had gotten their wires crossed about what kind of business we were here to talk about. I calmly rise to my feet and walk to the elevator. Mr. Creepy follows me, so my hand wraps around the pepper spray in my bag, ready and waiting for him, but the *maître d'* catches him and makes him pay for the dinner we never ate. I give the restaurateur a grateful look as the elevator doors shut. My grip on the small canister relaxes, and I withdraw my hand from my purse. Just because I could have handled him doesn't mean I wanted to.

When I get to the ground floor, I go to the valet stand and wait for the next available car service. I'd gotten a ride with Dad to the restaurant since there was a game tonight, and the arena is down the street. The match-up, which I'm proud to say ended in a victory, finished an hour ago. If I'm lucky, I might be able to catch him and get a ride home. I start to text when Todd barrels out the door of the hotel and storms over to me.

"Where do you think you're going?"

He grabs my arm, and for a weirdo with three drinks in him, I have to admit he has a powerful grip. He's also not a small man, so the teenage valets fade into the background, afraid of taking on a bigger, richer guy. I don't blame them. I'm not thrilled about this either. However, I'm not defenseless, having taken classes, so I know what to do in this sort of situation. I stomp on the arch of his foot with my heel, but either this guy has a wooden foot, I missed the mark, or an Old Fashioned is a fucking great painkiller because he's not bothered in the least.

Well, shit. Panic rises a little, which is stupid since we're on a busy street. But no one is stepping forward to help. He's got ahold of the arm that I'm using to hold my phone, so I grab at it with my other one.

"No fucking way," he snarls, knocking the phone out of my hand to skitter a few feet away on the sidewalk. This has escalated into scary in three seconds flat. Remembering my pepper spray, I shove my free hand into my purse, but it's over the opposite shoulder, the one he's holding on to, so it seems impossible to find.

He moves in as if to kiss me. I struggle to break his grip and stay away from his slobbery mouth.

"Let go of me. Stop."

He isn't listening and manages to grab both arms now in a crushing hold, causing me to gasp.

"Stop!"

A fist flies past my face and connects to Todd's chin, snapping his head back. His hold on me gives way as he falls and lands on his ass on the sidewalk.

He's fighting mad and battles to regain his feet until Brian Anderson steps next to him and knocks him back down with a foot tap to Todd's shoulder. "It's best to just stay down, or Caveman might live up to his nickname. Boy, did you pick the wrong woman to mess with."

Lincoln? Linc threw the punch? I spin, and he's right there. I throw myself at him, and he catches me, wrapping his strong arms around me as I bury my face into his chest. The adrenaline dump leaves me shaking and cold. I burrow closer, wanting his warmth.

"Bri, do me a solid and escort this asshole out of my sight." His voice rumbles through his chest.

"My pleasure." I hear feet shuffle on the concrete. "Come on, dickwad. Don't you know when a woman says *stop,* it's your cue to walk away?" Brian's voice drifts farther off as he continues to harangue Todd.

It's kind of funny, but I can't seem to shake the adrenalin still pulsing through me, so I'm not laughing. Besides, if I start, it might sound kind of hysterical instead of giggly. What would have happened if Lincoln and Brian hadn't come to my rescue?

Linc's hand strokes my back in long, slow caresses. "You're safe, I've got you."

I sigh. I can't hide in his arms forever, no matter how much I'd like to. Pushing myself a few inches apart, I stare at his handsome, concerned face.

"Are you all right, Catherine?" He reaches and tucks a few loose strands of hair behind my ear. "When I saw…" He shakes his head, and the hand resting on my hip gives a slight squeeze. "Did he hurt you? Maybe you should get checked out?" He glances around as if he'd spot an EMT waiting on the corner.

"I'm fine."

"You're still shaking."

"Adrenalin can be a bitch." I try for a reassuring smile, but by his frown, I didn't succeed.

"Ah, miss? Excuse me?" The squeaky voice of the underage valet breaks into our conversation. "Here's your phone."

"Thank you."

The glower on Linc's face has the teen scurrying away. I slap his shoulder. "Stop that. He found my phone. Don't give him scary looks."

"He should have intervened. Or at the least, got help."

"He's a kid, cut him some slack." I shiver again, thinking what a close call I had. Apparently, being on a public sidewalk surrounded by people, you still can't be safe.

"Hey," he takes my hand. "Let's get you home." He pulls me to his side, his arm draped across my shoulders, giving me his warmth.

"What were you doing here, anyway?" Normally, he'd be at MacKay's or home.

"Oh, shit. Hang on." He pulls out his phone and starts texting. I miss being in his arms already. "Zach pulled his captain card. A bunch of rooks decided to party at the Albion's bar." He looks away from the screen, gazing at me. "He sent me and Brian to look after them so they'd make the plane."

Probably a smart thing. I should let them carry on with their babysitting duties. "Oh, I can get myself home. No worries."

"Nope. Not gonna happen." A *ding* sounds, alerting Linc to an incoming text. He smiles and shows me the screen.

> Linc: Taking C home. U okay on your own?

> Brian: Good to go. I'll keep an eye on the kids.

"See, no worries. Where's your car?"

"At home."

"Perfect. Brian has his own. We drove separately. So let's get you home."

Okay then. He pulls me to his side, and we walk toward the public parking garage. If he's taking me home, he's coming inside. The adrenaline has me pumping still. The kiss on our date hasn't left my thoughts. Maybe this night doesn't have to end poorly after all?

X

I hand Linc his beer before sitting next to him on my couch. Requiring something stronger, I stare into my scotch before taking a sip.

"Thanks for coming in. I needed a distraction."

"Not really a hardship."

My right arm twinges and I absently rub my biceps. In fact, both my upper arms ache where Todd had grabbed me, but the scotch seems to help. And Linc's presence.

"Hey, are you all right?" His fingers wrap gently around my hand and pulls my fingers away. "You've been rubbing your arms in the car and here as well." He frowns and reaches for the sleeve of my blouse. He slips the buttons from their holes and rolls my sleeve upward. Just above my elbow, an angry black bruise comes into view. "Shit" He pushes the sleeve a bit higher before it becomes stuck. It doesn't matter. There's a spectacular bruise in the shape of a hand marking my skin, which isn't easy considering my skin isn't pale white but light brown.

With a growl, he does the same for my left sleeve, revealing a matching bruise. "Who is he? Tell me his name."

"Not going to happen."

"Oh yes, it will. I will track down that mother-f-ing asshole and—"

"Do nothing." I grab his hand and squeeze. "It's bad enough you hit him. He could have pressed assault charges."

He snorts. "No, he couldn't. There were a ton of witnesses. *You* should press charges."

"But if you go after him, he can. He's a douche, so he probably would."

"Fine. I'm not happy, but fine." He stands and pulls me along with him. "Go change. Take some ibuprofen, and when you get back, we're going to ice your arms."

"We are, are we?"

"Yep. I've got plenty of experience with treating bruises. Now go." He pats my ass before heading into the kitchen in search of ice packs.

No doubt about Linc and bruise expertise. After years of getting hit by ninety-mile-per-hour pucks and collisions with players, he's had lots of practice. I take the stairs to the fourth floor and wander into my bedroom. *Hmmm*, what to wear to entice him to stay the night? I rummage through my dresser drawers and smile when I find the perfect outfit. I strip down and pull on a pair of tiny, tight yoga shorts and then top it off with the spaghetti-strap, silky camisole—no bra. Entering the bathroom, I study myself in the mirror. Oh, yeah, the hair bun has got to go. I pull the pin, and my silky dark hair tumbles down where it lands mid-back. Much better.

Finding the ibuprofen, I swallow two pills before padding barefoot out of the bathroom, through my bedroom, down the stairs, and making my way to Lincoln. He is sitting on the couch, frowning as he stares at the two ice packs balanced on his knees. He hasn't noticed me yet, and when he does, I hope to make an impression.

"Hey."

His gaze snaps to me, and his eyes grow wide. He swallows hard and clears his throat. "Come here." His voice is a low rumble.

I saunter to him and stop, standing between his knees. He

pushes the ice packs to the side, reaches for me, and then tugs me down onto his lap. Perfect. Without a word, he picks up the first cloth-covered ice pack and wraps it around my right bicep. My left is soon covered as carefully.

"Why am I on your lap?" I think an actual growl escapes him. I smother a laugh.

"In that outfit, and with ice, you're going to get cold. I figured I'd keep you warm."

"There's a blanket," I gesture to the back of the couch. "I could wrap myself in that."

"Yeah, I don't think so." His arms curl around me, and he pulls me against his chest, tucking me into himself before resting his chin on top of my head. So far, so good. Hard to be sexy while wearing ice packs, but I doubt Linc will let me take them off yet. Besides, it's no burden being cuddled on his lap, and I have a feeling his need to hold me is more than about keeping me warm. He does have an overprotective streak. Seeing me being manhandled freaked him out. So it's a win-win in my mind.

He sighs. "Are you sure you're okay?"

"I'm fine. Promise."

We sit in a comfortable, companionable silence as the minutes tick by. It's nice being in his arms, but I have other plans. Enough time must have passed for the ice to do its thing. I'm ready to move things from cold to hot.

I reach for the pack's Velcro strap, but Linc's hand curls around my fingers. "It hasn't been twenty minutes," he rebukes me with a growl.

"I need something else." My statement catches his attention like I knew it would. I believe if it were within his power, he'd want to give me anything I'd desire.

"What do you need?"

I smile as I pull off the packs and toss them to the ground. Twisting on his lap, I straddle him. "You." My hands land on his cheeks, and I pull him down for a kiss. My lips press against his, and he groans. His large hands grip my hips as his tongue teases my mouth open. Warmth spreads through my body as our kisses turn heated. We make out like a couple of teenagers. It's even better than I remember. This man knows how to kiss. But I want more. My hands leave his face. One grabs his shoulder and caresses down his arm while the fingers of my other hand stroke through his silky hair.

I pull myself closer, and yes, he's into this. No mistaking his erection for anything else. We both groan as I rub myself against him. He kisses his way down my neck, and his hand goes wandering. His fingers dance along my side, grazing my silk-covered breast to my shoulder and then down my arm.

When his feathery touch crosses my bruise, I can't stop my flinch of pain. He immediately sits upright and stares into my eyes. "What am I doing?"

"Um, I thought that was obvious."

"You were assaulted tonight. This is the last thing we should be doing."

"I beg to differ."

A squeak escapes me as he stands with me, one hand under my ass and the other wrapped around my back. I tighten my legs around his waist as he strides away from the couch. "Our first time together is not going to be some adrenaline-fueled mistake, Catherine." He carries me up the stairs and then into my bedroom, where he gently places me on the bed. "Get some rest. I'll call you tomorrow when we land."

"Wait, you're leaving?" I rocket off the bed and grab his arm. My pulse is pounding, but no longer in a good way.

He stops, studying me with a slight frown. My freak-out must be obvious. I don't want him to leave. It's foolish. I know I'm safe in my own home, but right now, the idea of being alone isn't something I can do.

"Please stay. I know you have an early flight, but I don't want to be alone right now." I look down at my feet, feeling embarrassed.

His finger tucks under my chin, lifting my gaze to his. "It's okay. I'll take the couch downstairs."

I shake my head. "Can you sleep with me? I mean, really sleep. I won't…"

"Catherine."

"Please."

His sigh is my victory. "Fine. Get in bed. I'll be there in a second."

I watch him walk into the bathroom. "There's a spare toothbrush in the drawer."

"Thanks." He closes the door, and I stare at it for a moment before turning to my bed and pulling back the covers. I slide in, waiting for Lincoln. I don't have to wait long. He steps out and makes his way to the chair in the corner. Unbuttoning his shirt, he slips out of the soft cotton and then places it on the chair. Next, his shoes and socks go, then his pants.

He turns, facing the bed in only his boxer briefs. The man is built—broad chest with a slight dusting of dark hair over solid pecs and an eight-pack. His muscular thighs are huge and strong, calves tight, and there's something about a man being barefooted that completely works for me.

He chuckles. "Get a good look?" He strides to the opposite side of the bed and places his phone on the nightstand before drawing back the covers and climbing in.

"Um, yeah. But I doubt I'd ever get tired of the view."

"Hush." He pulls the sheet and blanket over us as he lies on his back. "Come here." He takes my hand and gives a tug, which I willingly follow. He pulls me into his side, and I snuggle in close as I rest my head on his chest. When he wraps an arm over my waist and hugs me tight, I can't help the sigh that escapes me.

I close my eyes as his body heat warms me, and his heartbeat lulls me into relaxing. With a long exhale, I fall asleep.

CHAPTER
Nine

LINCOLN

Still muzzy-headed after the plane takes off, I murmur my thanks to the flight attendant for the third refill of my coffee.

"Hot, strong, and black, just the way I like my men," Lacy Colton says with a wink. She's been flying with us on the team plane for years, so I expect some smart-ass remarks from her. Sonny smirks, and I know his mind has gone into the gutter with hers.

"You okay, old man?" Holt sneers as he struts down the aisle to the back of the plane, where the angry douche will sit in isolation. That happens when the team kind of hates him. He's the one who pushed us all away, though. When Holt was traded to the Quakes, both Zach and I tried to make him feel welcome, but the prickly walls he hides behind are unbreachable. "Did the rooks wear you out? Need a little nappy poo before we hit the ice? Someone posted a hysterical GIF of you asleep in the net being pelted with pucks. It's gotten over ten thousand likes so far, including mine."

Yeah, yeah. They got a shot of me after I poured water on my face, so my eyes were closed and then added animated pucks. I saw it this morning, too, with a bunch of Quakes' fans howling for my blood and very few supporting me. I've worked hard to let all that crap roll off my back, but to chirp at your own teammate on social media? Not cool. The dumbass doesn't even see me put my foot out, sending him stumbling into Ribi in the row behind me.

"Get off me, *bedak*," Ribs laughs, shoving the kid farther down the aisle. I have no idea what he said since it's in Slovenian, but his accent made it sound way too nice to be "asshole." He thumps my shoulder with a, "You go, Caveman," just as I'm raising the piping hot cup of coffee to my lips. Of course, the dark liquid sloshes out onto my suit pants, putting him on my shit list right next to Holt. I hold in the muffled curse as the burn sets on my thigh. At least my slacks are black, so the stain won't show in the team photos and videos that will be plastered on the Quakes' social media feeds of our arrivals and departures.

"Give the man a break," Sonny commands from across the aisle with a knowing grin. "He had a late night being a superhero."

Fuck. Brian must have told them about me taking Catherine home. Jesus wept, when did my teammates become eight-year-old hormonal boys? What pissed me off is they clearly think I'm the kind of guy who would take advantage of a woman. I put the coffee down and swivel to face Sonny, Ribi, and Bri sprawled out around me. "I'm going to say this one time. Fuck right off, all of you. I expect this bullshit from an asshole like Holt, so what's your excuse?" I pour on an extra helping of glare, but none of them break down in tears, so I give up, face forward, and gulp my now tepid coffee.

The truth is, I'm exhausted, but not for the reason their dirty little minds think. Catherine fell asleep almost immediately, but I spent the rest of the night wide awake, afraid that if I moved, I'd disturb her. Because if she woke and resumed grinding on my eager cock, I don't think I could have stopped myself a second time. So I lay there, staring at the ceiling, mind reeling about all the reasons pursuing this relationship is a terrible idea. Unfortunately, there were a few very compelling arguments in favor of it lying in my arms. The way she smelled like orange blossoms and spice, the soft silkiness of her hair splayed across my chest, the fierce look in her eyes as she fought back against the douchebag. They all add up to a woman I can't make myself walk away from. Not yet. Hell, with the trade deadline fast approaching, the choice of staying with her or not might be taken out of my hands altogether.

"Dude," Zach busts me out of taking residence in my head. "We're sorry. Obviously, you'd never do anything she'd wake up regretting. It's just you two looked pretty good together that day on the ice and at MacKay's. We want you to be happy, man, that's all."

"Whatever," I reply, but we've been playing together too long for my mates not to understand that means, "thanks, apology accepted." I recline my chair back as far as I can just to invade Ribi's space and nod off, dreaming about those kisses and the way Catherine tastes.

X

No matter where you play, in every city, there's always at least a small pocket of fans there rooting for you rather than their hometown team. It's a thrill to hear them, and tonight was particularly special as they started chanting, "Cavie! Cavie!" over and over again at the end as I brought home a big regulation win with a gymnastic clutch save. Only ten seconds remained on the clock. Their star forward pick-pocketed the puck from Mikey Cote and made a breakaway. He left our players in the dust and was joined by another of his, making it a two-on-one. Me being the one. But I held fast and made an impossible save in the last seconds. The New York Warriors would have tied, and they have the first-place league ranking of wins in overtime. Going into OT probably wouldn't have worked in the Quakes' favor. So we got two points, and the third-seeded team in the Metropolitan division got nil.

It's game four of our five-game road trip. Plus, the second game of a back-to-back. Dvorak played a hard-fought game last night against the current second-place team who is trying to rise in the same division. Considering the schedule, it had always been the plan for me to be in the crease tonight, giving Alexandr a break after I rode the bench for the last three games. And for the first time in a long time, I felt fantastic on the ice. My hip didn't twinge or ache at all. I was super loose, like my twenty-five-year-old self. I'm not sure if I'm energized again because I have something outside of hockey with Catherine. She brings a smile and happiness to me, even though we've only texted or chatted. I can't wait to see where things will develop with us.

After the big win, the boys did the usual goalie hug and helmet taps. But Raki came rushing off the bench, colliding with me in this running chest bump and then a Russian bear hug, which made me laugh. I want to hate the guy for stealing my job, but he's just so damn nice. I mean, the win isn't against the best team in the division, but the Warriors are ahead of the Quakes in the league standings. My game clicked into place tonight. I had no problems tracking the puck. Even with the body screens, I managed to have only two pucks slip past me. I made twenty-nine saves, and the last one was epic. It'll make the clip reels, for sure.

The press can't get enough of me after the game. Just yesterday, they were calling for my head on a pike. Today they're fawning over me and asking the dumbest ass questions like, "How did it feel to win?" How do they think it felt?

Do I look like someone having an existential crisis and pondering the meaning of life? It feels fucking fantastic.

Maybe it's all the blogs talking about how much better off the team will be once they trade me, assuming they'd trade me, that got me fired up. Or Tolli's pep talk. I'm not sure, but I played like the old me in the third period. The goalie who makes incredible saves which got us our second Cup.

But when Bri, Mikey, Z, and the guys from the second line invited me to go out for dinner with them to celebrate, it was a no-brainer. I had to pass. Physically and mentally, I was shot. Sure, it was the old me out on the ice, but the old me is *old*. Well, at least in hockey age. Thirty-six is ancient in this sport. Nothing went *pop* during the game, so that's a good sign, but the smart move is to rest and ice what ails me. Besides, the hotel we're staying at has an excellent room service menu, so I'm not missing much. Thank you, Manhattan.

The other reason to stay in, and if I'm honest, the more important one, is Catherine. We've been texting every day, multiple times, since I spent the night with her. She texted me after the game to congratulate me on the win. She wanted to hear all about the game. Would I be available for a video chat before we got on the flight to Winnipeg—our last stop on our ten-day road trip? I was so flattered that I suggested tonight. She didn't want me to miss the victory dinner and drinks with the guys, but I insisted. I eat half my meals with those giant oafs. Missing one dinner wouldn't kill me. Even with my first win in a fucking long time.

I'm dressed and almost ready to leave the visitor's locker room when Sonny and Ribi come over to me, concerned looks on their faces. "We heard you're not going to dinner. You okay?" Zach asked.

I panic a little, worried he'll do that captain thing and make me get checked out by the med team. Christ, that's the last thing I need now that I'm playing well, and getting benched for precaution will never happen again. I took a puck to my mask in the second period but shook that fucker off and cleared the concussion protocol during the second intermission. "Yeah, sure, I'm great. No need to worry your pretty little heads, I just…"

Well, shit. Do I tell them about the planned call with Catherine to get them off my back? They'll want to hear that more than I'm worried my hips might tighten if I sit down too long for dinner. Besides ice and ibuprofen, there are yoga stretches in my future.

"Look, if this is about the plane trip out east, I'm really sorry." Bri walked over and joined us. "It was stupid to tell anyone that you left with…" He glances around the locker room and must decide on discretion, "her. Neither of you needs that shit right now."

Yeah, my friend couldn't keep his mouth shut and told Zach and Luka about the fight with the douche and me taking our boss home. Not that I mind. The four of us are close, brothers from other mothers. They know I'm attracted to Catherine, hence the ice rink hijinks. I can't fault them for thinking she and I had sex. Well, maybe a little. But I forgave them, and I meant it.

"No, dude, it's all good. We're good. I'm not some angry Matt Holt holding a grudge. To be honest," I hesitate. I'm not sure what the upcoming call or all the texting even means, and I sure don't want word of it getting around, but these are my brothers. "To be honest, I'm having a FaceTime call with Catherine in about"—I check my watch—"a little over an hour. Which means I have to hustle back to the hotel to have enough time to eat before we talk."

"Ooohhh," they say in unison, smirks chasing away their concerned frowns.

"No, not, *oooohhhh*, it's not like that. At least, I don't think so. But you can't tell the other guys. I don't want to make her life difficult."

"You mean more difficult than dating a jackass like you?" Sonny laughs at his own joke, assuring me mum's the word as they leave.

Eager to get ready, I blow past the other stragglers and grab a ride share to the hotel. Normally, we'd have to take the team bus. With the win, management is looking the other way, with the understanding the players would meet curfew and be back in their rooms for a good night's sleep. Especially since there's a plane to catch in the morning for our flight to Winnipeg.

I can't stop grinning like an idiot. My play between the pipes had come together. Hopefully, tonight signals an end to my slump. I never want to lose five in a row again. And I get to see Catherine tonight, even if it is only on a screen, which makes me a double winner.

X

The hotels we stay at on the road are always sweet, but this one in New York is one of my favorites because of the food. The restaurant, like the city, is open 24/7, so even though it's near midnight by the time I get to my room, kitchen service is still available. First things first, I order a shit ton of ice to be delivered to my room. I'm desperate to call Catherine, but I'm stronger and more flexible than I've been in months, and there's no point in screwing with a system that's working. Plus, I know I need to eat to replace all those calories I spent during the game. So I order room service and then soak in an ice bath while I wait. Yes, God dammit, at my age, I need to keep the inflammation manageable. Everyone plays hurt, but I'm on a hopeful hot streak now, and if I'm going to keep making those saves, I need to be careful.

As an added bonus, if you want to call it that, my cock stiffens at the thought of calling Catherine. I'm like a teenager ready to explode, but when I get into the tub, the temptation to stroke myself vanishes almost as fast as my cock shrivels when I hit the icy water.

The kitchen must be busy, though, because I ordered before my soak, took another hot shower, and my food still hasn't come. I'm not one of those prima donnas who would grab the phone and shout, "Do you know who I am?" at the poor shlub on the other end. It's not like I didn't carb pack before the game, but the thought of a steak has my mouth watering. So I do a few yoga stretches, think about calling Catherine again, and—surprise!—Mr. Happy is back. At least I know I didn't break him in the ice bath.

Finally, there's a knock on my door as the delicious scent of meat and potatoes wafts into my room. I try to cover all of my excitement with the plush hotel robe, but there's no cloth thick enough to keep it under wraps. Fuck it. Opening the door a crack, give the kid a twenty for a tip and tell him to leave the cart, I'll bring my dinner in when I'm ready. I wait five seconds to be sure he's gone and then retrieve my food, checking to be sure the hall is clear before I wheel the cart in.

I would normally take my time and savor the perfectly cooked medium rare steak, but my cock is having none of it, twitching in anticipation of my Facetime call. My gut clenches at the need to get some release, so I wolf down most of the meat, strip off the robe, and climb between the crisp, cool sheets buck-naked. I grab my phone to call her and groan when my cock becomes erect and hard as nails. A drop of pre-cum appears on my tip, but I'm happy to find that even in my hockey dotage, I have enough control to hold out until Catherine answers. Because I don't know what she has in mind, but we are definitely both going to pleasure ourselves. I can't wait.

CHAPTER
Ten

CATHERINE

I stare at the phone in my hand, impatiently waiting for it to ring. Like a watched pot, I doubt it will boil any sooner by me staring. Pushing a strand of loose hair from my messy top bun behind my ear, I exhale in frustration. I wish he'd call already. Via text, we agreed it would be better for Linc to call since he was unsure when he'd get to his hotel room. I force myself to put my phone down, which in turn leads me to grab my wine glass.

The game started at four-thirty West Coast time. I curled up on my comfy gray sectional couch at home, having snuck out early to watch, and boy, what an exciting game. I knew he had to speak with the press, shower, then make it back to the hotel and eat. My clock now reads nine forty-five, which makes it almost one in the morning in New York. Could he have fallen asleep? I couldn't blame him if he did. He must be exhausted from the physical effort he put forth tonight. I chew on my lower lip, feeling conflicted. Should I call him? Maybe wake him for my selfish need to see him? Why is it that when it comes to Lincoln Cavanaugh, I always feel like an insecure schoolgirl? Especially when I'm anything but.

Walking into the kitchen, I grab the open bottle of red and pour the rich, dark wine into my glass. Suddenly, the distinctive warble of an incoming video call from my phone breaks the silence of my house. Ha! The moment my back is turned, of course, he calls. I rush across the room with glass in hand and grab my phone. A selfie of me and Linc flashes on the screen, making me smile. I sit on the couch, set my wine down, and swipe my phone screen, accepting the call.

Linc's gorgeous face fills my screen. "Hey."

"Hey, yourself, beautiful. I've missed seeing you." His greeting warms my heart, and just hearing his voice sets my pulse racing. It's been a week since he left, and though we've kept in contact, we haven't seen each other until now.

"I've missed you too." I give him another smile. "But it's so late in New York, and you've got a morning flight. Maybe we should postpone? You should go to bed. You must be exhausted."

"Not on your life. I couldn't sleep now, even if I wanted to. I'm in a weird place of being amped yet mellow. Besides, I'm in bed already." His smirk releases his dimple, and my skin heats with his innuendo.

I take a sip of wine to cool myself off. "You were amazing tonight." I'm dying to know about the game—every thrilling save and how he got it done. I want the professional color play-by-play from inside the crease. His game was phenomenal.

"Thanks, sweetheart. It felt amazing, but I don't think my gameplay is over yet. There's more to come."

"Of course not. You're a legend for the Quakes, I—"

"Catherine." His interruption in a low, commanding voice causes full-body tingles. I shiver. "That's not what I'm talking about. The game discussion can wait. You on your couch?" The heat in his steel-gray eyes turns me mute, so I nod. "Go to your room and get on the bed. Leave the wine. You're not going to need it."

My stomach flips with his growled order. Mesmerized, I can't seem to make myself move. He must take pity because he only stares back at me through the screen. How in the world did he know? Again? First, our food truck date, and now this? It's like he can see deep inside me. None of the men I've been with have ever figured out how much it turns me on to have them take charge. Yet he's staring in all his alpha male glory, believing he knows my secret. Which he apparently does.

As a high-level businesswoman, I'm constantly giving orders, always making every decision, and sometimes that pressure feels like a boulder on my shoulders. Don't get me wrong. I have a strong sexual drive, and there are definitely times I like to be in charge, but that's not my factory default. And I know it's not fair to the men I've been with to judge them for not figuring out my needs, especially when I don't tell them. But there's this starving part inside me, hoping for a man to innately understand. Lincoln Cavanaugh stuns me.

"Catherine, you all right?" I nod, still in mute mode. "We don't have to do anything you're not up for, I just..." And for the first time since the video call started, I see a flicker of uncertainty filling his expressive eyes.

Get it together! I can't let him doubt himself, not after he read me so clearly. "Um, I'm good." My words come out low and husky.

"You don't sound so sure." He gives me a teasing smile.

"I am." This time, there is confidence in my statement. We're going to have phone sex. A first for me. And I won't have to be in charge. A lightness spreads through me, making me feel bubbly and excited.

"Catherine." He pulls me away from my careening thoughts. "Get your sexy ass in bed, or there will be penalties."

I stand, gulp down the rest of my wine for fortification, dash up the stairs, and make my way to the main suite. "Are you going to put me in the sin bin?"

Linc chuckles. "Oh, there will be sinning."

I wasn't planning on having long-distance pleasure tonight, but I'm happy I'm in my normal PJs of yoga shorts and a camisole. Easy access for me. I'm not quite ready to get naked in front of him. I want it to be in person—skin to skin—for our first naked time so I can touch him. Reaching my bed, I fling back the blanket and sheets and hop in. With my back braced against a stack of pillows, I hold the phone to my face.

"Hi," I can't help my grin.

"Hey, beautiful." We stupidly keep staring at each other while smiling until his eyes light with desire. "Slide down and prop your phone on the pillow next to you. I want to see your face, but you're going to need both your hands."

"I am?"

"Yes. Do it now."

I shiver as I shift myself prone and put the phone on a higher pillow next to me. I turn my head and look into the camera. With this angle, he's seeing my face and the top of my breasts peeking from my camisole. "Is this good?"

"Perfect."

I can just make out his face and the partially revealed bare chest. There's movement of his shoulder and upper right arm. Is he…is he touching himself? I flush with heat and grow wetter with the thought. There's only one way to be sure, and I'm not shy. "Are you stroking yourself?"

With heavy-lidded eyes, he stares at me. "Yes. Does that turn you on?"

I swallow hard. His jerking off with obvious arousal, all focused on me? Absolutely. He's lighting me up. "Yes." A slight, knowing smile curls his lips.

"Catherine, slide your hand down and slip your fingers

into your panties." Almost on its own accord, my hand does as instructed. "Are you wet for me?"

I stroke my fingers through my folds. "Oooh…yes." Pleasure floods my system at the intimate stroke.

"Touch your clit. I know it's swollen and needy."

I find my magic bundle of nerves and stroke a feather-light touch, teasing myself. Arousal makes me wetter and hotter. A moan escapes me.

"Do it harder. Faster. It's what I'd be doing if I was there."

Lost in desire, I obey. My hips buck in response. I can't believe how close I am to my climax. It's never this fast.

"That's right, Catherine. Get there. I need you to come for me." Linc's arm is moving faster as his breaths come in harsh bursts. I wonder how close he is. "Pinch your nipple. Hard. Now." His order is growly.

With my free hand, I slide it into my top so he can see, and when my fingers clasp the tight bud. I squeeze harder than I ever imagined. I cry out as my whole body bows off the bed with the force of my climax, held rigid with the seemingly never-ending release. Finally, I collapse back onto the cool sheets, breathing hard. My eyelids flicker open, my gaze drawn to the screen just in time.

"Cat!" Linc shouts as his own climax hits him. I watch in fascination as he throws his head back, neck muscles bulge, arm and hand still stroking, as he milks his release for all his worth. Wow, that's super hot.

Lifting his head, his sated gaze locks on mine, as satisfied and content as me. He wears a contented smile, and his dark gray eyes turn warm. "You are so beautiful, Catherine, so fucking gorgeous when you come."

"You're kind of hot as well."

This earns me a chuckle. "I think I might be able to fall asleep now. How about you, sweetheart?"

"I could sleep." A welcome lethargy melts my bones and muscles, relaxing me into my mattress. I barely have the energy to pull the sheet and blanket to cover myself, but I manage.

"It's okay, beautiful. Go to sleep." His low, soft words lull me, and my eyelids close. "That's it. Let go. I'll talk to you tomorrow. Sweet dreams, Cat."

I drift off to the soothing, rumbly voice of Lincoln Cavanaugh.

X

"Thanks, Dean." I smile at Daniel's executive assistant. He had women in the past as EAs, but they never stayed for long. With a frustrated sigh, I leave my brother's outer office and pause in the hallway. He's dodging me.

Ever since the dinner with Todd Johnson—henceforth to be known as El Creepo—my brother has pulled a disappearing act. He's not answering my calls or texts. He's never home, much to his wife's dismay, when I've dropped by at all hours, and I haven't been able to catch him at Bishop Tech, like today. Poor Dean, he appears embarrassed and uncomfortable, giving me the brush-off. Daniel can run and even hide, but no matter how long it takes, I will confront him. What the hell was he thinking of leaving me to deal with El Creepo? I will have my answers.

While I'm here, I might as well check in with Dad. He's always so busy, and I like to offer my help on any projects so I can lighten his load. I know Mom will appreciate the extra time with him. God knows what Daniel has been doing for the company since it appears he's never in the building. I stride down the hallway to the corner office and stop before Martha's desk. She's been my father's right *and* left hand for the past twenty years, for which he's compensated her accordingly. Dad refuses to let her retire since he'd be lost without her.

"Hey, Martha," I smile at the sophisticated silver-haired lady sitting behind her desk. "Is the old man treating you well?"

She laughs at our shared joke. She's two years his senior. "Let me check, but he always has time for you." She grabs the phone and buzzes my Dad. "Catherine is here." Pausing to listen to his reply, she smiles. "Will do. Remember, you have a four o'clock conference call with Ancel Core." There's another pause. "You got it. I'll send her right in." She hangs up the phone and gestures to the door. "He has time, go on in."

"Thanks, Martha." I give a wave and head to the frosted glass and chrome double doors. Pulling one open, I slip inside and smile at my dad. The floor-to-ceiling glass windows offer a spectacular view of downtown L.A. They frame my father sitting behind his old-fashioned cherry wood desk. That particular piece of furniture is out of place in the modern, sleek decorations in the rest of his office. The walls and carpet are light gray, and there's a sitting area featuring a white leather couch and chairs with black pillows and accents. There's a chrome and glass bar, and on the other side of the large office space sits a glass conference table with matching steel chairs with gray cushions. It's all a complete contrast to his misplaced throwback desk. This office is a replica of his Quakes' corner office. Perhaps there was a two fer sale.

Robert Bishop stands and walks around his desk, meeting me halfway. I never realized until this moment, he kind of matches his office with his silver hair and blue eyes. I'm enveloped in a tight hug before he pulls back and gives my cheek a quick kiss. "This is a lovely surprise. Come sit. I have a few before I need to take that call."

He places his hand on the small of my back and guides me to the couch. I sit and sink into the soft, buttery leather. "I was trying to track down Daniel, but he's not here, so I thought I'd drop in on you."

A slight frown mars my father's face. "I haven't seen him around lately either."

Huh? What is Daniel up to? It's not like him to disappear, let alone long enough for our dad to notice. I make a mental note to work harder on tracking my wayward older brother down. Something isn't right.

"So, Catie, what can I do for you? Do you need something?"

My father's question draws me from my head, and I chuckle. "Actually, I was going to ask you the same thing. You've been working so hard lately I was wondering if I could help *you* out."

"Of course you are. Because running an NHL team isn't keeping your plate filled," he chuckles.

"I could say the same, you know."

"No need to worry. I've finally closed the deal on the microchips from the holidays. My plate is now bordering on empty."

"Yeah, right."

"No, seriously, I'm good. I even have a date with your mother tonight."

"Eww, don't want to hear."

He laughs. "Fine, oh, and I'll be at my fun office tomorrow." The *fun* office is our practice arena in El Segundo. Of course, my dad would think owning an NHL team is play. "Did Carter let you know about the meeting? He's going over possible trades and acquisitions."

Asshole. He did not. "No. What time?"

He sighs. "It's at ten. I'll speak with Geoff. He knows you're supposed to be in all these meetings."

"Good luck with that."

"So, at least I can gloat with an 'I told you so' about Lincoln."

On the road, Linc had gotten his game back. At least, it appears so. After returning from the ten-day away trip, he played twice more in the net unexpectedly. The initial opportunity came at the first home game. Dvorak had gotten slammed into one of the pipes holding the net in a crushing blow. Even though the net released from its moorings as designed, he was out for the rest of the game. Linc had come in as relief halfway through the third period and stopped all pucks shot at him. The latest, two nights ago, he had to fill the crease against the Washington Red Tails when unlucky Alexandr came down with a bad case of food poisoning just hours before the puck drop. He had another outstanding game and got another win. He now has three victories to his credit. Three more, and he'll cancel his slump. I am so thrilled for him. I hoped we could get together after his most recent win, but at the last minute, I had to go to San Diego. It seems fate keeps conspiring against us, keeping us apart. But not for long. I have a dinner date with him tonight.

"With Cavanaugh playing so well, which I knew he'd do, there's no reason even to consider trading him. Something sure has awakened his passion. He's playing like the Caveman we used to know. Any ideas? Love to bottle it and give it to a few other players, like Mikey Cote. He's been biffing the PK lately."

I blush. It's almost like Dad knows we've been fooling around. But it's not like we've actually had sex yet. It's just playful flirting and a hot round of phone sex. I mean, Brittany does more than this with her golf instructor when she goes for her lessons, not that she's a standard to shoot for. And, oh God, am I turning red? Because my dad chuckles at me.

"No idea, but it's great to see the Cavey of old back again."

"Oh, 'Cavey,' is it now? When you were so keen to trade him, it was Cavanaugh." Dad smirks.

"Dad," I scold, "a trade still makes sense. If he keeps playing well, we'll get more for him. He'll be one of the oldest goalies in the league next year, and we need to clear cap space."

Silence fills the air after my declaration.

"A player is more than his stats," we both say in unison. I've heard his catchphrase a hundred times before.

"You should make sure he knows how much we appreciate him."

"Dad?!" What the hell does he mean by that? I'm so embarrassed. Is it obvious how I feel? Or am I reading too much into his statement?

CHAPTER
Eleven

LINCOLN

"Now think, *grrrr*, like you were in the game a few nights ago."

What. The. Fuck. It's my time slot to do the photo shoot where they take the videos they'll use next year of us in the new retro sweaters, and all I can think is that Catherine's brother, Josh, is way too into this. Even the videographer and photographer give him weird looks.

We're on the ice using a green screen. Josh has taken over the promos, so it's different from any other shoot I've done. Usually, there's a simple logo backdrop. God knows what they'll project behind me when it's all said and done. He's been giving me instructions to look tough and scowl—which is easy because that's exactly the expression I want to make right now, but this *grrr* thing is new. I have got to remember to ask my boys about it.

"Come on, growl like you did right before you pushed that guy out of your way. Brilliant play, by the way."

I was in the crease two nights ago against Washington and

was pretty revved up. So I try to repeat the expression, but frankly, I feel stupid. After about half an hour of skating to the camera, looking over my shoulder, crouching down, and a bunch of other moves we'd no way in hell ever perform during a game, I throw my stick onto the ice in frustration.

"Josh, I'm not fucking Christian Bale, I have no more looks to give you." But the truth is, the more I shoot these promos for next season, the more I think, what's the fucking point? Odds are I won't be here next season, whether it's from being traded or retiring, so this is all a colossal waste of my time and theirs.

"Oh, come on, dude. Just a few more," Josh begs. "We're going to need these for next season, especially if you keep on playing like you are. No need to worry about the trade deadline." He chuckles.

My stomach rolls. The March deadline looms in less than a month. Ever since the road trip, my game has gotten better, but is it enough to secure my spot? Hockey, after all, is a business. I'm regretting not having a *no-trade* clause in my contract, but I never thought I'd need one. I thought I'd be a forever Quake. But I've got to say, I'm back in my happy place and blocking shots, which I've been missing since October. Maybe it was Jason Tolls giving me a different path. Maybe it's Catherine.

"Fine, you get one more, then I'm out of here." I glare at Josh for good measure as I skate out of frame. Catherine. I can't wait to see her tonight.

"Annnnnd, action!"

I skate to my mark, spin, and stare into the camera. My thoughts aren't growly and death to my opponents. They're about getting Catherine naked and in my arms. I want to kiss her all over, make her come, and sink deep inside her. After I feed her, of course. I'll be the gentleman first because later, I'm not sure when my baser instincts will take over, making me live up to my nickname.

"Cut!" Josh shouts. "That's perfect. It's a wrap. I have no idea what you were thinking, but your stare was intense."

If he only knew I was undressing his sister in my mind and visualizing all the dirty things I want to do to her. That might make things awkward. Glad I can finally get off the ice, especially before someone spots the wood in my pants and not the stick in my hands.

I stomp into the locker room and freeze when I see Holt inside. *Shit.* Just what I didn't need. At least the sight of him makes my chub disappear. I get my feet moving and stop in front of my stall, tossing first my stick and then blocker inside.

"I hate these fucking shoots."

My head swivels to Holt. Is he engaging with me and not leading with an age joke? I'll bite. "You're gonna hate it even more with Josh in charge. Best to bring a sense of humor if you want to get through it."

"Yeah, I don't see that happening."

Nodding, I have to agree. With Holt's anger issues, I fear for Josh. I pull my retro sweater over my head and continue to undress. So many pieces to a hockey uniform. On game day, it's like I'm putting on my armor, ready for battle. Not so much on publicity days. It takes an eternity to undress. At least I'm not overheated and sweaty from a game.

"So, um, Cavanaugh, you've heard the rumors? Read the blogs?"

I pause my undressing and turn, facing Holt. What the hell is going on? Is he trying to have a conversation with me? I study him, trying to figure out when he'll get stabby with a skate blade to my back because, with him, it's coming sooner or later. Holt has been a total asshole to this team. I have no idea where this is coming from, but he looks serious, even grimmer than usual, with his scowl and furrowed brow.

"You know, about trading you?"

"Kind of hard to miss. I'm sure you'll be happy to see me go."

"Nah, man. You're finally killing it in the crease. I just hate you when you play like shit."

Well, at least he's honest. And I still don't know what this conversation is about, so I keep silent and raise a brow.

"I didn't want you to be blindsided, I mean…" He rubs his hand down his face. "Fuck. Look, it sucks to get traded and not have any clue it's happening. I just…fuck, never mind." Holt goes back to getting dressed for his shoot.

His team traded Holt last season the night before the deadline. Could it be he hadn't known? "Matt, is that what happened?"

He pauses and stares me dead in the eyes. "I had heard the rumors…about me. I didn't believe them." Holt shakes his head. "The team and management were aware…there was a personal issue. I never in a million years thought they'd trade me. I mean…shit…it doesn't matter. Forget I said anything."

I stare a beat longer as he pulls the new sweater over his head. Shortly after he started with the Quakes, Holt disappeared for a week. The reason wasn't made public, and management simply told us it was a family emergency and left it at that, with no details. I only know when Holt returned, he was even more of a sullen asshole, which I didn't think was even possible. He also turned hostile on the ice, checking hard, laying guys out left and right, picking fights, and spending way too much time in the penalty box.

Matt grabs his stick and helmet. "Stop staring at me, fucker."

Annnnnd he's back. I watch as he strides out of the locker room. I wouldn't want to be Josh right now. It's never good to be on the pissed-off side of Holt. People get hurt. I shake my head and grab my jeans. The trade deadline has every player in the NHL on edge. It's that time of the year. If Holt felt like reaching out, maybe I need to think about my circumstances more seriously. I figured if I'm playing well, I'd be safe. Could be that's not the case.

X

My doorbell rings, making me smile. Catherine is right on time. I pad barefoot from the kitchen to let her in. Opening the door to my Manhattan Beach bungalow, I drink in the sight of her. Her oversized, dark chocolate sweater hangs off one shoulder, revealing her creamy mocha skin. Black leggings cling to her long legs—a favorite piece of her apparel I've grown to love. Form-fitting dresses that accentuate her breasts are nice, but I appreciate the stretchy yoga pants while spending alone time with her. I'm particularly fond of their shorter variation. Both hug her curves, highlight her legs, and show off her ass. I smile and gesture her inside.

This is the first time she's been to my house. It was a fixer-upper when I bought it several years ago after my divorce, feeling the need for a new space. Every offseason, my dad and I worked one room at a time. I'm pretty sure it was a way for my dad to make sure I was doing okay. Either way, if it was a mental health check or just father/son bonding, I'm pretty proud of how it came out.

"Welcome to Casa de Cavanaugh. Would you like a tour?" I chuckle. "It won't take long."

"I'd love one." She glances around my single-story cottage and gives it an approving smile.

"As you can see, it's an open floor plan." I gesture to the great room, which should probably be called a medium room because huge isn't descriptive of the space. The kitchen and family room are one area, separated only by a large island countertop. I managed to squeeze a small dining table next to the wall of glass with an inlaid set of French doors. The rest of the room holds a large couch and a big comfy chair around a driftwood coffee table in front of a fireplace. My sixty-inch TV is mounted above. I know, fire and electronics don't mix. Although it can get chilly at the beach, I work on the ice, so I rarely have much of a blaze in the hearth. "Down the hall is the main bedroom and guest room. There's a bathroom in the same hall for future reference."

"Good to know." She takes in everything from the recycled glass countertops and reclaimed white-washed hardwood flooring to the barely blue walls and the snow-white wooden beams crisscrossing the ceiling. "It's beautiful." Catherine turns to face me. "You did this all yourself?"

"My dad and I did most of it. Some things only needed a coat of paint. Others, like the old floors, needed to be completely replaced. That took us all summer one year, but it was satisfying working side-by-side with the old man, using refurbished wood from a barn that had been torn down. I'm glad you like it." And thank God for family because who knew what the color pallet would have looked like if my dad or I were left in charge. Guess where I inherited my color blindness? We both have red-green blindness, hence the blue-and-white vibe. Luckily, it works with the beach theme.

Placing my hand on the small of her back—because I can't go another minute without touching her—I guide her to the kitchen island and pull out a bar stool for her to sit on. She climbs up, and I head to the fridge. I pull out a bottle of white wine I'd opened ahead of time and pour her a glass that's waiting on the countertop. "Here you go."

"Thanks." She takes a sip and gives a little *hum* of approval. "I always pictured you as a beer guy. I would never guess you were such a wine connoisseur."

No need to tell her I called Eddie, who has a wine snob friend back in Quebec, to get advice on what to buy. Instead, I wield my killer smile and take credit by omission.

She gives the countertop smooth, circular strokes that

make me wish that caress was on my thigh instead. "This is unique. I've never seen this before. What's it made of?"

I study the bits of tiny colored pieces of glass in various shades of blue under the clear sealant. My sister, Valerie, assures me it's gorgeous, making me wish I could see all the color variations. To me, certain shades of blue appear red or green. "It's recycled glass. I did a lot of research and decided it would be a perfect fit for the bungalow."

She looks around the open space. "I think you could have a second career as an interior designer or at least a contractor."

"Ha. Nope. The color design was all the female Cavanaughs. But I wouldn't mind the building and fixing part. I learned to work with my hands as a kid, watching my dad. At first, it was a chore, like I hated having to help him make a dollhouse for my little sisters, but before too long, it became a special bond between us. Besides, I like taking raw materials and making something out of nothing." She gives me a knowing grin, and the heat rises to my cheeks. This is the most words I've strung together talking about myself in… well, ever.

She keeps grinning at me, and I finally break. "What?"

"Kind of like the way you take young hockey players and mold them into athletes."

Maybe all this trade talk has made me a suspicious fucker, but I'm not sure I like where this talk is going. "Have you been talking to Tolli?" I try to remain passive but narrow my eyes. Is she thinking of ways to soften the blow that they want to trade me but don't have any offers, leaving retirement my only option?

"Jason Toll? No," she laughs it off, and I'll be damned if the musical sound of her laughter dispels my dark mood, and I can't help but smile back. "I meant like you're doing with the Little Tremblers at the rink."

"Oh." Brilliant response, idiot. Fortunately, I'm literally saved by the bell when my kitchen timer goes off.

She gifts me a broad smile. "Something smells good."

"I hope you brought your appetite. I'm making linguine with broccoli, artichokes, and mushrooms in a white sauce topped with grilled salmon. Everything is done, just some assembly required."

"Wow, sounds delicious. You made everything yourself?"

"Don't sound so surprised. Yes, I did, including the sauce. Nothing but the best for you."

"I didn't know you could cook."

"Hold that thought." I slip out the door and head to the grill, where I grab the salmon filets and bring them inside. I start plating the dinner, adding first the homemade linguine. Next comes the veggies, topped with the white wine cream sauce, then the salmon steaks. Putting the dishes down, I pull out a chair for her.

I sit in front of my own plate. "I learned to cook as a teenager and found out I liked it. My mom worked hard for us, so when I could, I'd pitch in."

"Of course you did." Catherine takes a bite and chews. Her eyes close, and she lets out a moan that has me shifting in my seat. Yeah, I want to hear more of that, but not from food. "This is amazing, Linc. So delicious."

I grin. "Thanks."

We eat in comfortable silence for a bit before she asks a question I've fielded often.

"Don't get me wrong, this bungalow is beautiful, but I guess I was expecting a mini-beach mansion on the water?"

My two-bedroom, two-bath, single-story cottage is tiny compared to some of the players' houses, but I don't need much. "This fits my needs. I have a spare room if my family wants to drop in, plus since it was a fixer-upper, I saved a bunch of money." Well, the price of real estate in California is relative, and anything near the water is pricey. For most

people, my little diamond-in-the-rough might not be considered a bargain.

"It's not like you're hurting for money, Linc," she chuckles. "I do know your contract."

"True," I shrug, a little self-conscious. "It's just, I know I'm extraordinarily lucky to be living my dream of playing in the NHL, and I am aware of the sacrifices my parents made getting me there. So, I do what I can for my family. I've helped with college tuitions, home deposits, and emergencies. You know, that kind of stuff."

"Helped? Probably more like paid in full, didn't you?"

I'm not touching that one, so I shrug. With seven siblings and a lower-middle-class income, I'd do anything for my parents. And, of course, my brothers and sisters. It's the least I can do. Especially since I've achieved my dreams at their expense in the past.

The rest of dinner passes pleasantly with easy conversation and laughs. I've never been with a woman who I'm so comfortable being around. The more time I spend with her, the more my attraction grows. She's gorgeous, smart, and sneakily funny. I am so ready to raise the stakes. The make-out sessions, flirting, and phone sex were great, but I want more. Hell, I ache for more.

I dry my hands and then hang the dishtowel on the oven door handle to dry. Catherine offered to help with the dishes, but I shot her down. Most everything had been cleaned before she arrived, and the dishes left over went into the dishwasher. So I poured her more wine and told her to relax while I made quick work in the kitchen. I turn and find her standing in front of the French doors, staring into my compact backyard. It's small, but its vertical plank fence on three sides and carefully tended trees make it private and almost magical. *What? Where the fuck did that come from?* I abandon my weird musings and focus on Catherine.

Smiling, I stand behind her and wrap her in my arms. She

sighs and relaxes against my chest. Her amazing scent, which I've become addicted to, fills my nose, turning me on. "If the doors are open, and you can get past the traffic noise, you can kind of hear the ocean." I live a few blocks from the beach, within an easy walk, but I don't have an ocean view, not even from the roof. Too many taller homes in the way. I raise my hand and gather her hair in my fist, moving the long strands away from her neck and over one shoulder. My lips press to the satin skin of her throat. "Have I told you how gorgeous you are tonight?" I continue to press kisses along her neck as I lower my hands to grip her hips. Her skin tastes as wonderful as she smells.

"You might have." She tilts her neck, giving me more access.

"Hmmm, I've got plans for you," I mumble against her skin.

"I like plans." Her voice is husky and a little breathless.

"I'm going to make you come, and then I'm going to fuck you."

She shudders in my arms. I'm taking that as a green light. We've been building to this point, and we both knew where this evening would be heading. It feels like I've waited forever to have her naked in my arms. My hand grabs the lower hem of her sweater and pulls upward. Catherine helpfully raises her arms as I tug it over her head and off. Not looking, I drop it to the floor behind me. Peering over her shoulder, I take in the strapless peach lace bra, cupping her breasts as if lifting and shaping them for my pleasure. My hands smooth up her stomach to cradle her tits. They are a perfect handful as I mold and squeeze, enjoying her soft plumpness. She moans, and the sound goes straight to my cock, which she no doubt feels hard and rigid against her lower back. With a final squeeze, I release her to move around to her front.

Her bra clasps conveniently in front. I flick the interlocking bits apart, and the lacy fabric springs open and falls to the floor. Her breasts are perfect, nipples already tight pebbles. I lower my head, taking a tight bud of her brown nipple in my mouth. Her hands sink into my hair, and she groans. I give a playful nip before administering the same attention to her other nipple. Her hips push forward as I suck hard.

"Linc." My name is a plea on her luscious lips.

"I know, baby. I'll take care of you." I drop to my knees and kiss my way down her stomach. My fingers grip the elastic band of her leggings, and I waste no time pulling the stretchy cotton down her legs. I lift her foot, then the other, helping her out of the pants before I push them away to join her bra. She stands before me, wearing a scrap of peach lace covering her mound. A thong. My hands reach around and grab her naked ass. Oh yeah, she has a perfect ass—firm, with just the right amount of softness. I press a kiss to the lacey fabric covering her hidden treasure, already damp in anticipation, and inhale her musky scent. I can't wait any longer.

I peel off her thong and toss it aside. Staring from the floor, I take in a very naked Catherine. She's fucking stunning. I knew she would be. "You are so beautiful."

She smiles at me and runs her fingers through my hair. I want to purr when her nails scratch across my scalp. "I'm going to make you come all over my mouth and fingers." She blinks, and her eyes dilate with her arousal. I touch her calf and stroke my fingers to the back of her knee. I grip and pull her leg upward and drape it over my shoulder, opening her to my gaze. Her pussy is glistening for me, and I can't wait to taste, so I don't.

I lick across her folds, getting my first taste of her. Delicious. I think I've found my new favorite dessert. I dive right in, devouring her. My tongue slips into her entrance, and she moans, and then I move my attention to her clit. Teasing, I lick circles around the tight bud, making sure not to apply any pressure. She whimpers and presses her pussy against my face, looking for friction. I answer her unspoken plea. She's so wet, my finger easily slides into her, and I add a second, wanting Catherine to feel fuller. I stroke her while my mouth and tongue plays with her clit. A low groan escapes her throat, and her body begins to move in the rhythm my fingers have set.

"Oh God, don't stop. Please don't stop."

She has nothing to worry about. I'm not stopping until she comes. I curl my fingers and can tell I hit the magic spot inside her when her fingers dive into my hair, pulling, and her standing leg buckles. My free arm is tight around her ass, so she's in no danger of falling. She starts to shake, so she must be close. By the end of the night, I'll know all her tells and very much look forward to finding them. I suck on her clit, and she screams as her orgasm sets her alight.

I stroke and lick her through it, milking her release until she becomes dead weight in my hold. Smirking, I give her pussy one last gentle kiss before pulling away. I look up. Her eyes are closed, and she's breathing hard. Her mocha skin holds the faintest rosy flush. My cock twitches, and I'm so hard it's painful, but I don't care. She's so fucking lovely. I gently lower her leg. She wobbles a bit, so I keep a firm hold on her hips, waiting for her to show some signs of life.

Catherine's eyelids peel open, and she gives me a satisfied smile. I stand and kiss her. My tongue delves deep, reflecting how I took her pussy. I turn her and walk her backward, making sure to move us a few steps sideways so her back misses the wood frame of the French doors. I press her against the glass of the ceiling-to-floor wall. When I think she's capable of holding herself upright, I break the kiss and step away from her.

She's backlit by the fading sun. The warm glow is her own personal spotlight. I take her in. How the fuck did I get so lucky?

CHAPTER
Twelve

CATHERINE

I press my palms flat against the cool glass, holding myself upright. My body feels satiated, mellow, and flushed with warmth as I gaze at the irrepressible man before me. He's still dressed in a snug black T-shirt and ripped, faded jeans, barefoot and wearing a satisfied smirk. I know I just came hard, but looking at him standing there with an impressive bulge behind his zipper makes me ache. I lick my lips.

"Not fair. You have too many clothes on."

Linc's dimple flashes. Without a word, he reaches behind his neck and grabs his shirt. In the way guys do, he pulls it over his head and tosses it onto the floor. I'm not above ogling his broad shoulders, his chest with a light smattering of dark hair, and his rock-hard abs. Tattooless, which is rare for a hockey player. His left hand reaches into his front pocket while the right pops the button on his jeans and then lowers his zipper. I can't take my eyes off him when he uses both hands to push his pants and boxers down and off. He stands unabashedly naked before me, and he's glorious. His cock is erect and displays both an impressive girth and length, matching his overall build. He grips his shaft and gives a few strokes. My pussy clenches. There's nothing hotter than an aroused man who confidently pleasures himself.

I tear my gaze away and look into his gray eyes, filled with admiration and heat. I hold my breath and grow wetter for him. He opens his left hand, revealing the condom wrapper in his palm. Mesmerized with his sleight of hand, he has the foil packet opened and his cock covered in a blink. He stalks forward, looming over me, his hands landing on my hips.

"This is the fucking part. I promise to be a gentleman later."

A chuckle escapes me. "I'm up for that."

"Glad to hear."

With a startled squeak, I'm hoisted into the air by Linc's hold on my hips. His biceps bulge as he effortlessly raises me in a deadlift. I grasp his shoulders, and when he pushes between my legs, I curl my thighs around his waist. He presses against me, pinning me to the glass. Linc steals another deep, heated kiss before leaning his forehead against mine.

"I apologize in advance," he growls. "This is going to be fast and hard and over way too soon. I've wanted you for far too long."

Warmth fills me. My fingers push through his hair, and I pull his head away so I can see his eyes. "It's okay, Linc. I won't break." Dropping a quick kiss on his lips, I murmur, "I've been ready for this for a while now, too."

His fingers reach from under my ass where he'd been helping to support me and stokes through the wetness between my legs. "I noticed." He smirks. I shudder as he finds my clit. His touch disappears, and his arm is once again under me, tilting my hips forward.

"Line us up, sweetheart."

I reach between us, grabbing his hard girth. It doesn't take much since he's practically there already.

"Hold on." I quiver at his brusk command.

It's the only warning he gives me before he slams me down on his cock as he thrusts upward, lodging himself deep inside me. I gasp. Pleasure and pain flood my veins from his powerful invasion. My hands fly back to his shoulders, and my nails dig crescents into his skin. I tighten my legs around him. *Oh, God.* He fills and stretches me like no other man. His mouth locks onto mine, and his tongue invades me as deep as he does below. My tongue duels with his. This man can kiss. I squirm in his hold.

It must be the signal I've adjusted to him because he breaks the kiss and starts to right-and-proper fuck me against the glass. I'm more turned on than I've ever been in my life—both by his display of strength and desire. Sounds escape me I've never made before. He's powering into me, hitting all the right spots as I spiral upward.

"Linc. Yes." Heat courses through me, and pleasure pools low in my belly. With each hard, deep thrust, his body hits my clit. I can't catch my breath.

"Cat. Fuck." He takes my mouth again in a searing kiss while his free hand reaches between us. "Need you to come. Now."

He pinches my clit, and I explode. "Linc!" My scream echoes through his home. I thought my earlier orgasm had wrecked me, but I was wrong. Lights burst behind my eyelids, and all my muscles clench as erotic ecstasy swamps my body. Rapture in unending waves continues to flood me as he keeps pounding into me.

With one last thrust, lodging deep, his body becomes solid, rigid muscle as his own release hits him. His neck is thrown back, eyes clenched shut until he buries his face in my neck. I go limp, and somehow, he manages to hold me. We're both breathing hard, coated in a sheen of sweat, as we come back to ourselves.

I never imagined our first time to be against a glass wall, but I don't care if his neighbors took in the show. Lincoln Cavanaugh has outdone himself. I don't think I can move, so it's a good thing he holds me pinned, or I'd be a puddle on the floor. Is it okay I'm still turned on by his strength, even after experiencing the two best orgasms of my life?

He kisses my collarbone and then lifts his head, meeting my gaze. My breath catches. There is so much warmth and emotion in his eyes that I'm not sure what I'm seeing.

"Hi, beautiful." His dimple appears.

"Hey, handsome."

"You okay?"

"More than."

He drops a kiss on my nose. "Good to know." We both groan when Linc straightens to his full height and he slips from inside me. "I'm taking you to bed."

"I love this plan."

He kisses me. With me wrapped around him, he walks toward his bedroom. "I can do slow now. And long. It'll give me a chance to worship your body."

I shiver in his hold. I'm not sure I'll survive, but what a way to go. He carries me into his bedroom and gently lowers me to his enormous bed. The size of it makes sense. After all, Linc's a large guy. Reluctantly, I lower my legs, releasing my hold on his waist.

"I'll be right back." He turns, and I get a glorious view of his tight ass. Lincoln Cavanaugh is a work of art. He strides into the bathroom, no doubt taking care of the condom.

I decide to make myself useful even though the last thing I want to do is move. Feeling languid and loose, I force myself to stand and pull the comforter and sheet across the bed as far as I can reach without having to walk around the ginormous mattress. No blanket for Linc, and no wonder. He's hot not just in the looks department but in body temperature. I always run cold, so I can't wait to snuggle into his warmth, my own personal heater. Sleeping in his arms had been a joyous discovery. I slip back into bed, the cool top sheet a relief to my sex-heated flesh. Lying back, I rest my head on a pillow that smells deliciously like him. My eyes close as I take in the scent of a woodsy forest. I'm unsure if it's from his shampoo or body wash, but I love it.

"Hey now, don't fall asleep on me. Remember, I have plans."

My eyes flutter open, finding Linc standing above me. He's grinning, holding a strip of unopened condoms. Dear Lord, he *is* going to kill me. He tears one square from the bunch and tosses the packet onto the pillows next to me, placing the rest on the nightstand.

"I love seeing you in my bed." There's a possessive tone in his statement. His large hand first rests on my stomach before sliding to my hip and down to my thigh. He squeezes my leg before tugging my thigh, spreading me open. He climbs into the space between my legs. "I like having you here." He leans down, pressing my body into the mattress, and kisses me. His fingers thread through my hair as his other hand props next to my shoulder, taking some of his weight so he isn't crushing me.

Our tongues tangle. There's no sense of urgency like before. The kiss is slow and deep, as if it could go on forever. I shiver as desire floods my body, heating me to my core. Linc's hard cock presses against me, and I can't help myself when I rub against him. He breaks the never-ending kiss with a chuckle before he drops a kiss on my nose. "We'll get there, just not yet. You're finally in my bed, and I'm going to take my time. I want to find all your spots and maybe discover some you don't even know." He rubs his nose against mine before taking my mouth again, but this time in a blistering kiss that heats my blood.

He breaks away, trailing kisses across my cheek to my neck and up to my ear, where he sucks my lobe into his mouth. His teeth scrape before nibbling on the soft flesh. A whimper tears from my throat.

"That's one," he whispers into my ear. He works his way down my neck with open-mouth kisses, his tongue tasting my skin until he reaches the juncture where my neck meets my shoulders. He bites, and my whole body shakes. "Two."

He's driving me crazy. My core is throbbing for him. "Linc, please." The bastard chuckles again, and then his talented mouth and tongue are playing with my nipple as his hand cups my other neglected breast. His teeth clamp down on my rigid flesh, and my body arches as my hands fly to his head, fingers gripping the silky, thick locks of his dark hair. He releases my nipple and kisses his way across to my other breast. His hand strokes down and slips between our bodies.

He bites my other nipple as he thrusts two fingers inside me. I moan. With a *pop*, he releases my breast. "Three, four." He's apparently a biter, and who knew I'd be so turned on by his sharp nips? He slides off my body, so he's lying next to me. My gaze is drawn to his handsome face, and I realize he's staring at where his fingers are sunk deep inside me. I follow his gaze, fascinated at his muscled forearm flexing as his fingers begin to work me. He's hitting my G-spot, and I can't stop myself from moving. My hips sway in time with his stroking rhythm. The languid fingering has me climbing to the crest.

His thumb finds my clit, and I press into the contact, seeking more friction. "Can you come for me?"

"Yes." The word is a hiss. I'm so close. My heart is pounding, and heat pools low in my belly.

"Come, Cat. Come now." His command is all I need as I tip over the edge.

"Linc!" My whole body curls with the force of my release, and he milks my orgasm for all its worth. My body unclenches, and I collapse back to the mattress. When I can finally open my eyes, I find him rolling a condom down his hard shaft, and then he's kneeling between my legs once more. He strokes his cock against my pussy as we make eye contact and then notches himself at my heated entrance. Leaning forward, bracing his hands on either side of my shoulders, he sinks into me inch by slow inch until he's as deeply rooted as he can get. His smile is devastating as he leans down, stealing a kiss while allowing me to get used to his invasion. The man is big all over, and I haven't had sex in a while.

"You feel amazing. So tight. So hot. You're strangling my cock." I squeeze my inner muscles, making him groan. "You're not playing fair. I want this to last." Who wants fair when he fills me so completely? I need him to move.

I shift under him, seeking more. "Linc." His name is my wish, which he grants. His hand slides to my thigh, where he lifts my leg, hitching it high on his body, allowing him to sink deeper inside. We both moan as I curl my raised leg around him and dig my heel into his back. He finally moves.

His rhythm is lazy, pulling almost all the way out and then sinking deep. So different from our first time, but just as hot. I grip his strong biceps, looking for an anchor. The build to our release is a slow burn. He fucks me, and it's like time stands still. Ten minutes pass, maybe twenty? I have no idea as I float in our erotic dance, wishing we could stay here forever. But of course, we can't. His rhythm increases the closer we get to our mutual satisfaction. As before, he has me go first, and my release rolls through me. He follows right behind. His face burrows into my neck as he shouts his pleasure into my damp skin.

Linc lifts his head and captures me with his gaze. We catch our breath while staring into each other's eyes. His look holds both warmth and lust. He kisses me leisurely before dealing with the condom. Returning, he climbs into bed and pulls the covers over us. He spoons me, with his heavy arm draped over my waist, his hand landing on my breast. His face nuzzles into my neck.

"I love how you smell. How you taste."

This man. I turn and kiss him. He squeezes my body before breaking the kiss. I face forward, my eyelids closing on their own.

"Get some sleep. I'll be waking you for round three." He whispers.

I shiver and then snuggle back into his warmth. He has awesome plans. I fall asleep with a smile.

X

"It's been that good, huh?"

I blink and face Brittany as I realize I've been staring blankly off into the distance across my balcony with a smile. "Uh, *good* doesn't really describe it."

"Hot, damn." She raises her blood orange margarita in a toast.

I clink my matching drink against her glass. It's Friday, and we're having cocktails around the firepit on my balcony since Linc is keeping curfew by himself before tomorrow's game. I'm in such a good mood, I didn't want to be alone, so I invited Brit to hang out. We're munching on chips and guac while our delivery keeps warm in the oven. The late February evening is a gorgeous California night. We sit in front of the crackling flames, listening to the waves crash in the distance. I know she'll want details. Sex with Linc has been mind-blowing and special, a treat I selfishly kept to myself these past weeks.

"Deets, girlfriend, or your newfound sex life isn't real."

I sigh. We've been intimate for two weeks now, and I've been on cloud nine. Brit and I chatted, but this is the first time, with both of our schedules, we've been able to get together in person. We're busy, and now, with my relationship with Linc, my free time has almost disappeared. Stalling, I gulp my margarita.

"Hey." Brittany places her hand on my knee and squeezes. "What's going on? You know you can tell me anything, right?"

"I know"—I pat her hand—"It's just…I'm confused. Well, not confused, but it's complicated?"

"Then he's not doing it right." She laughs.

"Oh, no, he most definitely is doing it right." Brit raises an eyebrow, and it's my turn to laugh. "He always puts me first. I've never had so many multiple orgasms in my life. Linc is amazing."

"Yeah, multi's aren't a myth, at least with the right guy."

I sip more of the strong margarita—the only way Brit knows how to make a drink. She's not wrong. I've had good sex, but Linc has nothing on good, he's phenomenal. It's uncanny how he can play my body. "Brit, I'm kind of scared."

"What? That your sex drought has ended or about Linc?"

"Neither. And thanks for pointing out I'm much more selective than you are." She laughs at my teasing. My best friend has a high sexual drive and has never been afraid of a one-night stand. My smile slips off my face. I really don't want to admit this, but I need advice, and Brittany is the closest thing I have to a sister. "This was supposed to be a fuck him out of my system, have some fun, and wave goodbye when he's traded thing."

"Annnnnd?"

Ugh. She's going to make me say it. "I care about him. I'm emotionally involved." I chug more margarita.

"Well, he is kind of hot and lots of orgasms, so not so unexpected. Especially since you've always needed to have feelings for a guy you take to your bed. It's your MO. I'm not seeing the problem."

I set my empty glass down, wanting to go in for a refill but needing to get this off my chest more. "I don't think we'll trade him after all. His game has been so exceptional he's now playing in tandem with our other goalie. He's in the net every other game and still winning. The Quakes are on a streak that's about to break franchise records."

Brittany tilts her head with a thoughtful expression. "Are you sure a trade is off the table?"

I nod. "My dad has been against it from the start. The GM, on the other hand, is excited. He's getting offers for Linc with teams in desperate need of solid goaltending who are trying to make a bid for the playoffs. It's good business sense, but I don't think my dad will sign off on it."

"So in this version of reality, Cavanaugh, the giver of orgasms, stays."

"Yes."

"I'm still not seeing the problem here. You're finally having amazing sex. The cobwebs in your pussy have been well and truly cleared, and you'll be able to continue having orgasms past next week. Women worldwide wished they had your problem."

I stare into the flickering flames, unable to meet Brit's gaze. "I'll be a role model. The first woman to own an NHL franchise. If it comes out I'm fucking a player, not only will I be a laughingstock, the damage to other women wanting to break through the boys' club makes me feel guilty and humiliated."

"Ah, sweetie, being a female in a boys' world, I get the pressure, but you're missing the obvious."

My gaze is drawn to hers. "I am?" I think of myself as pretty intelligent. I've gone over my situation in my head hundreds of times since I got together with Linc. I can't think of what I'm overlooking.

"Catherine, you're not the owner of the Quakes."

A chill chases down my spine. "But I will be."

"Has your dad told you when he's handing over the

reins?" I shake my head. "Until he does, you are *not* the owner. No glass ceilings to collide against. No judgment. Only many, many, many orgasms."

My whole body stills, and I forget to breathe. Holy shit, Brittany is right. Maybe I can stay with Linc? My heart races, and I finally gasp in much-needed air.

"Plus, fuck 'em. I'm so sick of the double standards. If Elon Musk can fuck his assistant, you can have an affair with a player, owner or not." She stands, pulling me up beside her. "We need refills, and I could eat." She strides away, entering my house.

Grabbing my empty glass, I stare at where she disappeared. Hope infuses me. I've never felt this way about a guy before, falling in deeper than I dare admit. I was kidding myself that I could have a sexual relationship with no emotional ties. My best friend knows me better than myself. There was no way I could share my body with Lincoln unless there was some intimate connection. I'm not built that way, and she knew it.

I amble toward the sliding glass doors leading into my living room. Ever since I discovered the sport of hockey at my father's knee, a part of me knew I wanted to own a team. Another shiver chases through me. Is Linc worth risking the career I've dreamed of since childhood? I need to search deep for the answer because a part of me thinks no one is worth it, but the other half can't see me giving him up.

CHAPTER
Thirteen

LINCOLN

I swing, and my club makes a satisfying *thwack* when I connect with the golf ball. It sails through the air before landing dead center on the farthest target. My fist pump of victory is in rhythm to the blaring music and is met with groans inside the Topgolf bay behind me. I turn, grinning at my friends. I love it when I win.

Walking to the rack, I slide my club back into my bag and accept the fist bumps I deserve for beating their collective asses. It was so sweet when Topgolf opened a branch in El Segundo, making it super convenient for us to stop by after practice. The facility has three levels of all-weather bays, not that it's necessary here in California. It comes with a bar and food services. The many high-tech golf games ranging from beginner to advanced make this hella more fun than your normal driving range. It's particularly handy if you don't have time to play eighteen holes. My boys and I are hooked. It's a great place to blow off steam. Which, at least for me, is greatly needed with the fast-approaching trade deadline on

Friday, only four days away. I think my game has improved enough for me to stay, but as Holt pointed out, you can't take trades for granted.

I grab my beer and take a swig as I check the score on the HD screen mounted in the backfield behind the targets. We talked the facility into showing an East Coast hockey game. The perks of being a professional athlete are awesome. The Buffalo Tracers are duking it out with the Minnesota Frost. Of course, I'm rooting for my hometown team. I went to Frost's games for as long as I can remember until I left for college. Sometimes, I make it back during the season and catch a game with Dad, but that's rare with my schedule. Right now, they're kicking the Tracers' butts. Go, Frosts, go!

A pretty redhead brings another round of drinks and snacks for us, placing them on the table. She's been giving Luka the "I want to jump your bones" look all evening ever since she first laid eyes on him. In fact, on her way out of the bay, she brushes by him, and then he slips his hand into his pocket.

"Did she pass you her number?" Brian calls out. I guess I'm not the only one to notice.

"What can I say? Once I hit puberty, I never had to work for it. The ladies come to me." He chuckles and gestures to his body. "Life is easy when you look like me." Our Luka's face alone has melted women's panties at first sight.

"I'm sure the accent doesn't hurt, either," Zach comments dryly.

"Don't be jealous, Sonny. After all, no one tied you to the same woman forever." He points a finger at him. "You did it to yourself."

Zach nods. "Yes, I did. And I'd do it all over again in a heartbeat. Jenny's it for me."

I raise my beer and clink with Zach's. I'm always amazed at our Captain, how he can remain at the top of our sport and be madly in love with his wife and make it all work. Of course, now I think of Catherine. It's like she's re-awakened my youthful energy and focus. It hasn't escaped my notice that since starting whatever we have going, my play has completely turned around. I guess feeling like a fucking hormonal teenager again is great for my game. Maybe that's how Sonny does it.

The guys and I are taking a break before the next game. We reserved our third-floor bay for two hours. We can afford to relax with no pressure of being kicked out. Brian walks over and nudges my shoulder with a finger.

"So, speaking of one-woman relationships, how's it going with Catherine? You've been pretty hush-hush, ditching us on the reg, so I'm gonna assume it's because of our hot boss."

Brian's question draws the attention of the other guys, and now, a semi-circle of expectant faces surrounds me. I grab a pretzel bite and tumble the tasty treat between my fingers, mindful of the fact that I make my living with my body. While some goalies can be upward of two hundred and twenty pounds, my hip requires me to make sure it's all muscle and not carb-induced flab. Still, biting into the doughy goodness, even knowing it will take hours on the treadmill to compensate, seems worth the trade if eating means I don't have to talk. God, I wish I didn't hate the monotony of the treadmill so much. I'd rather run on the beach, taking advantage of California's perfect weather, but the sand is tough on my joints. Games of football, volleyball, and Frisbee are fine, but full-out cardio running for miles is a no-go. Thank God the team spares no expense, and we have a fleet of high-tech, shock-absorbing treadmills. They make a world of difference to my workouts. Wow, what a way to mentally stall.

I want to tell them everything that's been happening these past weeks since we've become intimate. To shout from the fucking rooftops how happy Catherine has made me. And it's not just the sex. I've never stayed awake until two in the morning debating Japanese noodle bowls versus California

Poke. The one thing she asked of me was to keep our relationship a secret. My career, whatever is left of it, would survive, but she's starting on her path. Her reputation would be in tatters if anyone found out about us. On the other hand, these are my brothers. Fighting for each other isn't just another day at the office. It's a way of life. She doesn't know they already figured out we're involved. I suppose I'm lying by omission, but if she asks, I'll tell her the truth.

"Oh my God, would you look at his face?" Zach shakes his head, but a shit-eating grin lights his eyes. "For the first time in the ten years I've known you, you're finally in love. And don't give me that Rainbow bullshit. That was an itch you scratched instead of getting cream to treat it. You are fucking in love." I wish I felt half the joy he does, gaging from his loopy smile.

"So why aren't you happier, Caveman?" Bri asks, sharing none of Sonny's glee. Playing the role of team psychologist as usual.

"I'm tired of keeping what we have hidden. It might be love because I've never been so fucking happy before. But I've also never felt so bad. She needs to keep our relationship secret. I understand, I really do, but it's hard not to think she's ashamed of me or something. I can't even tell my family, and we talk about everything."

"Have you talked to her about it? No one is a mind reader. If you're unhappy, tell her. Figure out some sort of compromise." Wisdom like that was the last thing I expected coming out of Luka's mouth. Zach's right. The accent makes anything sound better.

"Shut it, Dr. Freud. Let's change the subject." After selecting a new game on the console, I grab my club and head to the tee line. Zach cuts in front of me, laughing. He sets and strikes his ball, nailing the green number six. At least, I think it's green. I turn to Brian. "Was that green?"

"No, man. It's orange." He's serious for a whole second

before he can't help himself and busts out laughing. Luka high-fives him. Meanwhile, Zach keeps hitting section numbers on the green circle, racking up the points. Fuckers, all of them.

"Next time," Luka suggests, "we need to bring our sticks to play. Everyone knows Zach can't hit shit using his hockey stick."

He chucks a pretzel bite at Luka, who eats it. "Ha, ha. You guys got any summer plans?"

I smile, and the heaviness of the Catherine conversation lifts from my shoulders. "Tolli mentioned player development. I may help him coach some of the Tsunami during the off-season." Nobody asks if the plans will change if I'm traded, and frankly, I don't know either.

"Clearly, Zach will come to your camp to learn puck handling," Luka says with a charming smile that threatens to make a passing waitress swoon. "Me, I'm volunteering for a literacy program. Since I speak Spanish, the Quakes Foundation recruited me. Because you Neanderthals speak only one language, while I'm a citizen of the world and can converse in five."

We all laugh at his trash talk. He's not wrong. Our Luka is smart, a lady-killer, and one talented hockey player.

"Jenny and I might go to Spain. Teach me a few useful phrases."

"*Otra cerveza, por favor.*" He replies in a perfect Spanish accent.

"I'm pretty sure that's universally known, asshole," Zach retorts.

"Hey Rib, who will you be working with? Is the teacher hot?" Brian asks. We all smirk, although it seems to me Luka's merriment is a little forced.

"No idea. The Foundation set it up. It's a brand new program, so I don't have a lot of information." He sighs. "I kind of want to go home for a visit, but I don't know the schedule yet."

I take my spot at the tee. What if Luka is right about having a conversation with Catherine? I'm becoming obsessed with the idea of telling her how I feel. Because, at first, it was sort of fun sneaking around. Now it's like I'm her dirty secret. And isn't that stupid? I hit another ball, getting in the yellow five slot I need to pull ahead. Hopefully, that's a sign from God.

X

I stride through the corridors in the team's practice center, carrying the bag of takeout. The food is from Catherine's favorite sandwich place. Luka is right. How should she know what I'm thinking if I don't tell her? So I'm bringing her a surprise late lunch to her office, hoping to have a heart-to-heart.

Though her door is closed, I already have the 411 and know she's at her desk and hasn't eaten. It's two in the afternoon. She has to be starving. With a brisk tap on her door, I wait for permission to enter. I'm taking a risk here. The times we've met for lunch have been out of the office, in places far enough away where no one from work would spot us. This is sort of a litmus test—will Catherine bend a little or shut me down? This will allow me to figure out how I can broach my concerns.

"Come in."

Here goes nothing. With a deep breath, I open the door and cross the threshold, careful to shut it so I hear the lock click behind me. "Hey, gorgeous," I raise the brown takeout bag. "I thought I'd feed you."

Both her eyebrows lift, widening her eyes as her mouth dips into a slight frown before her expression morphs to neutral. Apparently, I catch her by surprise, and not necessarily a happy one. She stands, although how she manages to rise so gracefully in that pencil skirt and heels is beyond me. I can jump off the ice from the splits, and I couldn't manage her lithe move. Just thinking about her strong legs makes me tingle in all the right places. Then she leans a hip against her desk and crosses her arms against her chest. Not the body language I was hoping for, and all signs of happiness down below melt away. She's hard to read, with her relaxed stance but closed-off position. As my old man says, nothing worthwhile comes easy. I keep my smile and prepare to fight for us.

"Hi. Um, this is a surprise." She smoothes her perfect hair, captured today in a business-like bun, as she looks at the closed door and then back to me. She crosses her arms again.

I stroll closer and place our food on her desk before invading her personal space. Lifting my hand, I gently cup her face. "I missed you." I place a quick kiss on the corner of her delectable mouth.

"Linc—"

I press a finger to her lips, halting her words. Her eyes narrow, but she doesn't push me away. "It's just lunch." My hands fall away, but I keep our bodies almost touching. Only her arms hugging herself keep us apart.

"You kissed me."

"That was barely a kiss. I was saying hello."

A sigh escapes her. "We're at the office, Linc. You know this isn't right."

"Hmm, agree to disagree?" I gesture to her seating area. "We can sit separately. You take the couch, and I'll sit in the chair. If someone stops by, it's no big deal. It's not like we'll be caught having raging hot office sex." Although, dammit, now that I said it, the idea is turning me on.

She continues to stare at me, wearing a slight frown.

"I brought your favorite. The turkey, mozzarella, kale pesto, panini from Sofi's. You have to be hungry. Come on, take a break and eat"—I lean my forehead against hers—"please?"

She breaks away from me and returns to her desk, putting four feet of glass and steel between us as she sits. Snatching a random paper from the scattered files and pretending to read it, she grinds out, "I…we had an understanding about keeping our relationship private." Her cool, calm demeanor doesn't fool me. From the way the vein on her temple jumps, I know she's pissed. I fight to keep my temper under control and take a seat across from her. The food might be forgotten, but no way I'm going to let her ignore me.

"I hear your concerns, and I understand why you're afraid to go public about us," I say in my calm voice that I use with the Tremblers when they're scared of getting hurt. It works like a charm on the kids but has the opposite effect on Catherine.

"Oh, you hear me, do you? Then why are you in my office in the middle of the day, where anyone, including fucking Carter, can see us? Because that's just what I need right now in the middle of fighting him over trading you, for him to see us together."

Deep breath in, deep breath out. I draw on the discipline I use in a game to ignore all the chirping and shoving from the other team, looking to distract me so they can score. I'll get back to the topic of still trading me later. Because…What. The. Actual. Fuck? Tamping down my anger, I take another breath. "First, I checked. Carter is in Ontario for the game, watching some of our up-and-comers in the Tsunami."

"As if none of his little snitches will call and tell him about this," she fires back, interrupting the speech I had prepped in my head, throwing me off my game. Damn, it's a good thing she doesn't play on an opposing team. She's doing a better job derailing my calm than any chippy player has in a long time.

"Second," I continue as if she hasn't interrupted me, "I

asked your assistant, and you don't have any meetings scheduled, so there's no reason for anyone to come barging in."

"You what?!" Her face flushes with color like she's about to orgasm, but I'm guessing not. "Did you make an appointment with her? Ask her to block off an hour so I can give you a blow job?"

"What? No." Okay, maybe calling her secretary was a mistake, but it's not like she recognized my voice or anything. "I mean, unless that's an option?" I pour every ounce of charm I have into my smile.

"No, that's not an option," she hisses, shooting me with a laser glare.

"Okay, that was a joke, just in case that bun is pulled so tight it's cut off the oxygen supply to your sense of humor." *Dial it back, or you'll screw your mission*, the voice inside my head tells me. Too bad my heart has decided to take the reins. "Look, I haven't felt this way about anybody in a long time, and I'm sick of being treated like I'm your dirty little secret. You don't want to go public, you want to keep it from everyone, you want to be fucked into ecstasy and then sneak off so no one knows. What about what I want?" I get to my feet, breathing hard now. Dammit, that sounded a lot less sappy and confrontational in my head, but it's still true.

"Linc, don't do this—"

"This? Have a discussion with you?" I run my fingers through my hair before gripping the back of my neck. "When you gave me a second shot, you made me promise to talk to you if I was upset or angry." I gesture at myself. "This is me—talking."

"Come on, that's not what I meant. Your silent treatment is childish."

"Really? Because I'm getting the distinct impression you'd rather I keep quiet. Jesus, Catherine. All I want is to have lunch with you and a conversation. Why do my needs matter less than yours?"

She plants her hands on her desk and pushes her way to her feet, glaring back at me. "Because your need to be the cock of the walk and show off that you bagged the owner's daughter *isn't* as important as my need to keep the career I worked my ass off to get. Don't kid yourself, Cavanaugh. Orgasms are a dime a dozen, but this job is my dream."

Her words rock me to my core, my pulse pounding in my ears. Was it all about sex to her? And dammit, I want to hit something to get my man card back. "Oh yeah? Well then, dream on, lady, the ice suits you." I cross the room, yank the door open so hard the knob embeds in the wall, and stalk out in search of the nearest beer.

Unfortunately, I never make it to a bar. I didn't even get to my car before my cell rings. I don't recognize the number, but answer it anyway. At least it's a distraction from my swirling thoughts.

"Cavanaugh." I'm really hoping it's a sales call so I can let loose some of my anger on the unexpecting salesperson.

"Lincoln, it's Carolyn. Carolyn Barth."

She's one of the coaches for our teenage league. Like the Tremblers are for the littles, the L.A. Junior Quakes are for teens. A branch practices here in the afternoon after school.

"I heard a rumor you're in-house. Are you still here?" A rumor? Which might prove Cat's point that coming in was dangerous. *Fuck.*

"Yeah, CB. I'm in the parking lot."

"Oh, thank God. Greg called, and he has to stay with his son, who was sent home from school, sick. I could really use a hand."

I grip my neck. Normally, I'd say yes, but teenagers are perceptive. They'd easily catch on to my less-than-stellar mood. And there's Catherine. I'm not sure if I can be in the same building with her.

"Please? Pretty please? There's a bunch of setups for

today, plus me corralling and working with twenty-five hormonal teens. I could really, really use your help."

I sigh. I'm a fucking sucker when it comes to women. "Sure." I turn around and enter the practice center. "I'll change and lace up. See ya in ten?"

"Yay! Thank you so much. You're the best."

I only wish Catherine thought so well of me. At least mentoring young hockey players is my safe place. It might ease this ache in my chest and the sadness that is steadily replacing my anger. I can't believe she wouldn't even hear me out. I guess our relationship wasn't a thing.

I sigh. It was to me, though. Our romance happened fast, it's only been two months, but I have fucking feelings for her, falling hard. *Idiot*. How am I supposed to deal with this emotional crap? Hockey. I'll lose myself in the game I love.

CHAPTER Fourteen

CATHERINE

My bribe of great seats to the remaining home hockey games seems to have worked. Dean, Daniel's EA, sent me an email letting me know my brother will be in his office at six tonight. After my fight with Linc, I'm in the mood to punch someone—it might as well be my older brother. I need to confront him and find out what the hell is going on with him.

Ever since Linc stormed out of my office, my concentration has been shit. What was he thinking? I had to remove the food he brought because I had no appetite, and the sight of it made me sick to my stomach. So, I hid behind my closed door, getting nothing done until it's time to head to Bishop Tech and find out what the hell is going on with Daniel once and for all.

Standing, I grab my purse and charge out to the parking lot. It's a sucktastic time to travel from El Segundo to downtown L.A., but what's a girl to do? The seventeen-mile trip should take about twenty minutes in a normal city. In Los Angeles, during rush hour? It will take me a good hour. I'm hoping to arrive by six-thirty, optimistic Daniel will be settled in and I can catch him unaware. But since I have no idea how long he's planning on staying, I'd rather get there a little earlier. Fingers crossed, the traffic gods are with me.

I hop into my Subaru BRZ and go play in traffic. Blessings are bestowed upon me because I reach Bishop Tech way faster than expected and park in my reserved spot in the garage. Two spaces over, I spot Daniel's white Camaro ZL1, so he's definitely here. In the building's lobby, I show my ID to security. Bishop Tech is only one company among several occupying this downtown highrise. Once through security, I catch an elevator for my ride to the thirtieth floor. Since it's technically after hours, I have to scan my badge to gain access to Bishop Tech. There will be some people still working, but the front reception leaves at five.

I stalk through the corridors and arrive at Daniel's office. I don't bother knocking, but barge right in. Luckily, he's only sitting at his desk and not screwing someone on top of the African Padauk wood behemoth. I've heard rumors that's what happened more than once, sometimes after office hours, but sometimes not. I feel sorry for Shannon, his wife. When did my older brother become such a douche?

"What the fuck!" Daniel startles at my surprise entrance.

"Doing some actual work, I see." I stride forward and stop in front of his desk. "Why have you been dodging me?"

"I haven't." His eyes dart away before meeting my gaze. *Liar*. I raise an eyebrow, waiting. "Fine, I've been busy and didn't want to deal with your bullshit."

"My bullshit?"

"Yeah, yours." He frowns. "What the hell, Catherine? Todd told me Lincoln Cavanaugh punched him, and then Brian Anderson dragged him away. You're lucky he didn't press charges and fuck the team."

My mouth drops open, but I snap it shut. "Those players came to my defense. He was trying to force himself on me—"

"Why do you always have to be so dramatic? Has it been so long you don't get it when a man hits on you?" He throws his hands in the air. "I thought I was doing you a favor, but no, you had to almost break the guy's finger and set your hockey goons on him."

"A favor? What the fuck are you talking about?"

"I told Todd you could use a good screw."

"You what?!"

My brother chuckles. "I figured if you finally got laid, you might lose that stick in your ass and chill out."

Wow. I'm speechless. Daniel had me meet with El Creepo, thinking I'd sleep with him. He's lost his ever-loving mind. "If that's your idea of a favor, please don't do me anymore."

"Well, you can do me one." I keep my mouth shut and glare at him. "Step away from the Quakes. They should go to me anyway, as the oldest and a man."

"What? Since when are you interested in the team?"

"Obviously, you can't be in charge. You couldn't keep the players from assaulting a person on the street. If Dad ever found out—"

"He'd thank Linc and Brian."

"Ha, dream on. Even he can see you don't have the chops to run an NHL franchise. There's a reason there are no female owners. Just step away, Catherine, because you're going to crash and burn."

Where is this coming from? I know he has dirtbag tendencies because he cheats on his wife, but what is this toxicity about? "Daniel, what's going on? Is something wrong?"

He shakes his head. "Everything's fine."

"Really? Because you haven't been at Bishop Tech in days, others have been covering for you."

"It's called delegation. And I am working." He gestures to his desk with papers and his laptop.

"Well, something is going on. Owning the Quakes has been my dream since I was a kid, and now you want me to walk away? What is wrong with you?"

"You, Catherine, are what's wrong with me. It was fun to humor you when you were little, but not so much now. You need to step aside and let me take over."

"No. Never."

"I'm sorry you feel that way." He stands and glares at me. "I hoped you'd be reasonable, but I guess I'll have to play hardball."

"What are you talking about?"

"I've been prepping my case to convince Dad I should be the next owner. When I'm done, he's going to drop you so fast you'll have whiplash. Fair warning, I know what you've been doing."

My pulse races, and there's a boulder in my stomach. There's no way he knows about my relationship with Linc. He can't.

"Under-minding Geoffrey Carter, spreading lies about him. I applaud the underhandedness of it all, but it won't work."

Relief floods me so quickly I have to lock my knees to keep from collapsing. "Lies? He's a misogynist asshole, and that's the truth. He's so gone when I take over."

"So not happening, sis. I'm teaming with Carter to take you down."

"Dad will never allow it."

"I wouldn't count on Father. One way or another, you're out. You have my word. I will make it happen."

Staring in disbelief, I wonder what has come over him. I've noticed a change in him these last few months. This Daniel doesn't resemble my brother of old at all. Something more is going on, and I vow to get to the bottom of it.

"Game on, Daniel." I spin on my heels and storm out of

his office. He'll never take the Quakes from me. I won't allow him to destroy my dream.

X

Curled on the couch, I stare at the melting container of Ben & Jerry's Americone Dream sitting on my coffee table and stab into the center with a spoon. I still have no appetite. The yummy ice cream is going to waste. I should put it back in the freezer. The knock on my door startles me out of my reverie. I wasn't expecting anyone.

Part of me hopes it might be Linc trying to talk to me again, yet I'm not sure I'm ready to face him. The knock comes again. I can't ignore it. With my car in the driveway and the inside lights on, whoever is at my door knows I'm here. I should really install a door cam. Sighing, I get off the couch and cross the room. I peer through the peephole and am surprised to see my younger brother standing there. I unlock the door and swing it open.

"Josh, what are you doing here?"

"Hey you," he smiles a charming grin and brandishes a bottle of wine. "I bring wine, fantastic company, and distraction."

"How did you…Never mind, it doesn't matter. You're right. Please, come on in." I step from the entrance and gesture him inside. My little brother occasionally has ESP, and when that fails, he has an awesome spy network. I'm assuming he's here about Daniel, but for all I know, he's found out about Linc and me.

He heads straight to the kitchen, placing the bottle of Sangre de Dioses from Roblar—a favorite of mine from the Santa Ynez winery—on the counter, along with a blue file folder.

"Get the glasses," he commands as he plucks my wine

opener from the drawer. Making quick work on opening the rich red, he's ready to pour when I put the glasses down. "Here you go." He hands me a generously filled glass before snatching his own along with the folder. He marches to my couch and sits. Spotting the melting container of ice cream, he shakes his head. "Catherine, letting that go to waste is a crime against humanity." He grabs the treat, digs in with the spoon, and helps himself.

I sit on the opposite side of the couch and take a healthy sip of wine. Not wanting to get into my fight with Josh, I deflect. "What's in the folder?"

"Ah, the distraction first, I see." He puts down the ice cream and opens the folder. The file contains multiple 8x10 color photos. He pulls one out and hands it to me. It's Linc, in hockey gear, wearing next season's retro jersey while holding his helmet. His gorgeous face is on full display. He's staring into the camera with an intense combination of a scowl and a wicked grin. I know that look. It's the expression he wears just before he grabs me and fucks me. *Dear God*.

"That is one super hot man."

"Josh, you know he's straight, right?"

"I'm allowed to look. After all, I'm only human." He smirks. "One day, I'm going to find myself a hunky gay hockey player and check one off my bucket list. I'm so proud of our Jacob Novak for stepping out of the closet. He's showing the world that a third-line centerman can be openly gay and kill it on the ice. I could get down with him."

"No, you can't. He's still with Kyle, so no poaching."

My brother huffs a sigh. "Statistically speaking, there's got to be a few more of them out there."

"What happened to Mark? I thought things were great?"

"Eh, not so much. We broke up."

"Oh, bummer. I'm so sorry, baby brother."

We both sip wine. It must not have been a bad break because he doesn't seem upset, and I've been there for his many heartbreaks.

"Speaking of brothers…"

Ah, this *is* about Daniel. "How did you hear?"

He gives me a small smile. "If I tell you, I'll have to kill you."

Ha. So it was one of his spies. It's not like we were quiet while arguing, and I had left the door open to his office. I sigh. "I'm worried about him. Something's not right."

"There are several things not right. But I'm more concerned about him believing he can take the Quakes from you."

"He can't."

"Duh. Everyone, including Dad, knows it, so his insanity is worrisome."

"He's threatening me, and I'm not sure what to do. Should I go to Dad? He has enough on his plate already. I feel like I should handle this myself."

"Yeah, leave Dad out of this." Drinking more wine, Josh stares at me with concern. "I fly under Daniel's radar, but you've always been Dad's bright, shiny joy, making him resent you."

"He shouldn't. Dad loves us all,"—I shake my head—"but Daniel is acting way weird."

"Shannon is leaving him…finally."

"Oh my God." I'm stunned. Josh and I have both spoken with her about Daniel's cheating. We love her and couldn't stand it anymore, yet when given the facts, she still stood by her husband. "I'm both happy and sad for her. I need to make time to talk with her."

"His behavior could stem from his wife divorcing him, but my instincts say more's going on."

"Agree. I mean, you probably know about him ditching work." Josh nods. "But did you hear about a *supposed* business meeting he dumped me with?" I proceed to fill him in on El Creepo and my confrontation in Daniel's office.

"What a dick move." He grabs my hand and squeezes. "I'm glad you're all right."

"Me, too."

"Soooo," he smirks as he draws out the word. "Lincoln Cavanaugh, huh? The handsome hottie came to your rescue. Lucky girl."

Dammit. Heat flushes my face, and even with my darker skin, he'll zero in on my blush. I glance down into my almost-empty wine glass, but it's too late.

"I knew it!" He claps and practically bounces on my couch.

"You did not."

"I do now." Laughing, he pulls me into a hug, almost spilling my wine.

"I hate you right now. You can't tell anyone," I mumble into his shoulder before pulling away and downing the rest of my wine. "Besides, it doesn't really matter anymore. I'm pretty sure we broke up this afternoon."

"Wait, what? You've been so happy. What the hell happened?"

If we're having this conversation, I need more wine. Putting my glass down, I stand and go to the kitchen, grab the bottle off the counter, and bring it with me. I refill both our glasses and plop myself back onto the couch.

"Uh oh. What did you do? Your body language reeks of guilt. Spill it, sistá."

And so I do. How we found out about our mutual attraction, how Linc finally asked me out, our first date, and how phenomenal the sex was, without going into details. I even explain my fears and why I wanted to keep the relationship secret. "This was supposed to be a fuck him out of my system before we traded him, but no, I had to develop feelings, and he's not going anywhere. Why can't I be more like Brittany? Maybe it's a good thing we're on the outs. It would have never worked in the long run."

"I'm not surprised Brittany gave you bad advice. You are nothing like her man-eating ways. Plus, I don't think all hope is lost."

"Well, it should be. I can't be an owner who's fucking a player. I'd be a laughingstock in the old boys' network. Linc wants to go public, and I just can't."

Josh pats my knee. "I can't believe you didn't talk this out with him."

"That's where I feel guilty." I sigh. "I kind of lost my shit and said some pretty unforgivable things." I can't meet my brother's gaze. "I love him." My words come out in a whisper. "I wasn't supposed to fall in love. Now I've hurt him, and it's probably for the best because I can't be with him."

"Oh, big sis, you're breaking my heart."—he pats my knee again—"It doesn't have to be all or nothing, C. I think there can be a middle ground. I don't want you to throw away your chance for happiness. After all, he won't be a player forever."

He's right, but I can't see a compromise. Lord knows I've given it a lot of thought, ever since I realized I was falling hard for him. "I don't know what to do."

"First, you need to apologize. Second, offer him a tradeoff. Let him tell his family. And his close friends, though I'm sure they probably know and have kept quiet for both your sakes. Let him bring you lunch to your office because, truly, what harm can come from having lunch with a friend?"

"What about Daniel? If he finds out, he'll go straight to Carter."

He nods. "The thing is, you need to stay ahead of the story. Control it. Say, post a pic on social media of you and some of the guys on the team celebrating together. Use the boys as cover. Show yourself as a warm human being who spends time with her players. That doesn't necessarily tie you to Linc."

That could work. Relief floods through me as I see the light at the end of this long, dark, lonely tunnel. Then I realize it's an oncoming train. "But isn't that still lying? Pretending to be something we're not? How is that going to satisfy Linc's need to be open about our relationship?"

For the first time in our lives, I see a darkness flash behind my baby brother's eyes. "You're talking to someone who has a little experience pretending to be something they're not. This isn't the same. Look, Linc asked to have lunch with you, not do a photo shoot and plaster your faces on the cover of *InGoal* magazine. He doesn't want the attention any more than you do, he just wants to sit near his girl once in a while and not feel he has to be hidden away."

"In the closet?" I ask, wondering if, when I was away at college, Josh had something happen. It wasn't like our family wasn't aware and supportive of who he was, but it occurs to me now that maybe the world at large wasn't always easy for him.

"Something like that. You'll never know until you talk to him."

"Damn it, baby brother. When did you get so smart?" I grab him in a bear hug before I muss his hair. "You're a way better confidant than Brittany."

"You're welcome." Smiling, he stands and grabs the file folder. "Now, go to Linc and sort your shit out. I want you to be happy."

I stand and give him another quick hug. "Thank you, Josh. Wish me luck."

He pats my shoulder. "You don't need luck. I've seen the way that man looks at you. He'll forgive you."

I can only hope that is true.

X

It's ten o'clock, and I stare at Linc's bungalow door. He's inside because there's a home game tomorrow. It's the last game before the trade deadline the following day. Now, if I can only will myself to knock, it would be a step toward his forgiveness. I'm startled when the door opens, and Linc stands before me in sweats and a T-shirt.

"Are you going to stand out here all night?"

How did he know I was here? That's when I spot the phone in his hand. He must have a doorbell camera, and it alerted him there was a person stupidly standing on his porch staring at his door, all stalker-like. I swallow hard before clearing my throat. "Um, can I come in?"

He stands there and stares before finally saying, "Sure." He steps back, giving me room to enter. Thank God. For a moment, I thought he might slam the door in my face. I go to his couch and sit. When he approaches and sits in a chair instead of next to me, I know I'm in hot water.

"First, I owe you an apology. I'm so sorry. You are absolutely correct, and I was wrong. Of course, we could have talked." I get lost in his dark gray eyes. "I also regret the things I said to you."

He runs a hand down his face. "Then why did you say them?"

"I was scared...am scared." Looking down, I stare at my clasped hands in my lap, ashamed of how I treated him today.

"Can you answer one question for me?" Glancing at him, I nod. "Was it just sex to you?"

Shit. I really hurt him. "No, Linc. It was always more than sex. I'm so sorry I was such an asshole. You mean a great deal to me. I'm...I'm falling head over heels for you." My first tear trails down my cheek. "I'm scared. I love you, and I don't know how to be with you and still follow my dream." More tears follow the first. I can't keep from crying.

He stands and crosses to the couch, where he sits and pulls me into his lap. His strong arms wrap around me, and I bury my face in his chest. I feel so safe in his arms while I get myself under control. It doesn't take long. I pull away and wipe the remaining tears from my face. "Can you forgive me?"

He presses a soft kiss to my temple. "Of course, because I love you too. But we still need to talk." I nod as warmth flushes me, knowing he loves me as well. Then my stomach growls so loud his eyes go wide. "When was the last time you ate?"

"Breakfast." I glance away, not able to hold his gaze. "I haven't really had an appetite."

His fingers grip my chin, turning my face so I'd look at him. "New plan. I'll feed you while we talk." As if on cue, my stomach growls again. He stands with me in his arms and carries me to the kitchen before bending and placing me on a kitchen stool at his counter.

"You realize I can walk all by myself, right? You don't have to carry me everywhere."

He shrugs and heads to the fridge. While Linc takes out a Tupperware with leftovers and starts reheating, I decide to take the bull by the horns and start. "I'm really sorry for my freakout. And to be clear, I hate not being able to even be near you when anyone else is around. Not telling my parents about the most important relationship I've ever had. I didn't see a path forward without hurting my dream." A chuckle slips out. "Well, until earlier this evening when I actually got some pretty awesome dating advice from Josh. It's kind of funny since he's a serial dater with more ex-boyfriends than Trevor Rayne has one-night-stands."

He raises an eyebrow as he places a plate of chicken, rice, and veggies before me. "What? I know the locker room gossip. It's common knowledge number twenty-three is the team's manwhore."

"Eat."

I pick up a knife and fork and dig in because I'm suddenly starving, and the food smells fantastic. He places a glass of water next to my plate, wearing a slight smile as he watches me chow down. After I make a good-sized dent in my dinner, he dives into the conversation.

"So, what exactly was Josh's advice?"

"A compromise. First, tell your family. Of course, it's okay. I trust they'll keep the news to themselves." I sip some water. "He also pointed out that having lunch with a player in my office isn't cause for a scandal. Please feel free to feed me whenever you like." His dimple pops out, and the stress I'd been holding lifts from my shoulders.

"Baby, that sounds great. I don't want to be the hot topic in every locker room in the league either." He pulls me in for a slow, sweet kiss, and I sigh into his mouth. And then I remember.

"The bigger problem right now is Daniel."

I explain about our fight and finish with his threats to take the Quakes away from me.

"He can't do that." Linc is indignant for me. "I'd love to beat the fucking shit out of him." I straighten, about to beg him not to, but he holds up a hand. "I won't. I promise. However, it's probably for the best if we're never in the same room together."

"Thank you." I reach for his hand and squeeze it. He grabs my empty plate, rinses it, and places it into his dishwasher. "Josh also gave a suggestion to negate Daniel by getting ahead of any rumors. He thinks we can use the team as semi-camouflage by having more than just the two of us in public."

"Huh, that's not a bad idea. I'm sure the guys would love to help out."

I stand, realizing how late it is. "I should probably go. You've got a game tomorrow."

He rounds the counter, and before I can say another word,

he grabs my ass and lifts me. Instantly, I wrap my legs around his waist and clutch his shoulders, laughing. There he goes, carrying me around again. He walks toward his bedroom. His display of strength always turns me on. Maybe that's why he does it.

"You're going nowhere tonight." He smirks at me and then drops me on the bed. "We just confessed our love for each other. Besides, make-up sex is the best."

"You've got a game. You need sleep."

Linc chuckles. "I promise you a win tomorrow."

I guess it's makeup sex for the win.

CHAPTER
Fifteen

LINCOLN

The whistle blows, signaling the end of morning skate. I pull off my helmet and drop a glove so I can push my sweaty hair off my face. It was an optional skate since we have a game tonight, but in the NHL, there's really no such thing as optional. It's an unstated rule. Grabbing my glove off the ice, I corral my equipment and skate for the exit. As I get close, Coach O'Ryan signals me to wait.

"What's up, Coach."

"Mr. Bishop wants to have a word with you."

And right there, my gut clenches. The fucking trade deadline is tomorrow. Shit. Is he personally going to tell me I'm gone? Usually, it's the GM's job, but Bishop thinks of us as more than numbers, so this could be it for me. I try to console myself with my belief Catherine would have given me a heads up, but maybe even she didn't know until the last minute.

"Shower and then get your ass to his office."

"Yes, Coach. Will do." I hustle off the ice and into the

locker room and start the complicated process of gearing down.

"What did Coach want?" Brian asks during his own undressing routine.

I keep my voice low. "Robert Bishop wants to see me."

Brian's eyes go wide. "Fuck man, you don't think…"

Shrugging, I keep pulling off pads. "I can't think of any other reason."

"He found out about Catherine and is going to give his approval?"

I shake my head at his attempt to lighten my mood. Last night, she said she wanted to let her parents in at some point but was careful to keep Daniel in the dark. But she promised to give me a heads up when she did, so there'd be no surprises. If anything, it could be that the asshole brother made good on his threat and caused trouble for Cat. "Look, I've got to hustle. Can't keep the owner waiting."

Brian pats my shoulder. "Good luck. I'll tell the guys."

"Thanks." I grab a towel, wrap it around myself, and hit the showers. I speed through, and when I re-enter the locker room, I can't mistake the worried looks from my friends. Tuning them out, I dress and head for the stairs instead of the elevator. I need to burn off some of my stress. At the admin level, I stride to the corner office.

When I enter the outer reception area, Julie, his long-term EA, smiles. "Good timing. You can go straight in."

"Thanks, Julie." Taking a deep breath, I enter Robert Bishop's Quakes sanctum and close the door. The man himself stands from behind his desk and gestures to the seating area.

"Thanks for coming. You got here faster than I expected. How was practice?" He smiles and sits on the white leather couch. I take a chair, nerves flooding my system as my foot taps silently on the plush carpet.

"Good, sir. We're ready for tonight."

"Excellent. And it's Robert, not sir."

I'm sweating bullets. Our fourth line center got hurt in our last game. They had to cart poor Rue off the ice on a stretcher, never a good thing, and on top of that, we lost. The trade rumors have been flying. The newest is about a Canadian wunderkind the Quakes are expected to trade me for, plus two draft picks to get him. I don't want to leave this team. I don't want to leave Catherine. Hockey business can be a bitch, and it looks like I'm the latest to get slapped.

"I wanted to talk to you about two things. I know you're in the crease tonight, so I want to quash any rumors you might have heard. We are not trading you, Linc. You'll stay a Quake for life if I have my way. I wanted to reassure you so you can keep your head in the game. We need the win, especially since we're close to having home ice advantage for the playoffs."

Halle-fucking-lujah. The adrenalin dump that flushed my systems at the start of his statement releases so fast I'm lightheaded. "Thank you, sir—"

"Robert."

"Robert. I can't say I wasn't concerned. I really appreciate you taking the time to personally let me know."

"You're welcome. As I said, I can't have anything interfering with your play, especially since you're on fire." He smiles. "No thanks are necessary. You mean too much to our family." He pauses.

What. The. Hell? Is he talking about Catherine and me? No way. As far as I know, no one outside of our circle knows how serious our relationship is. It's a pretty tight group. And the only other Bishop family member included so far is Josh. I can't think she'd let her dad in on it without telling me.

"You know, the hockey family, the team and all," Bishop smirks, and I swear there's a twinkle in his eye. This man isn't stupid. He's a self-made billionaire. Why do I get the feeling he's playing me? I decide to change the topic.

"Ah, so you said there are two things?"

Robert nods. "With Nathan Russo on the injured reserve, we're pulling from the Tsunami."

"Who's getting the call?"

"Ansel Ricar. I understand you've worked with him?"

The kid is going to be a powerhouse in the NHL one day. That's why when Eeks needed my help, I reached out to him and gave him a taste. He's hungry. Rickie is going to be ecstatic.

"Great choice. I'm assuming he's getting the shot at center?"

"Yes," Bishop rubs his hands together. "I have a favor. I know it's Zach's job as captain to lead our team, but I'd appreciate it if you could also give the kid some special attention."

"Absolutely. The kid's a talent."

The good ones who get called up do one of two things their first time on ice—they show the world what they got, or they get in their own way and crash and burn. No way will I let that happen to Rickie. He's going to have the game of his life.

Speaking of life, here's my chance to feel out if the Quakes would have a place for me if I retire after this season. I grab the back of my neck and squeeze, forcing the words out. "So, sir, um, I realize you must be busy, but if you can spare me some more of your time, I wanted to talk to you about something." If he says yes to giving me the player development spot, I would at least know I have a serious option if I retire. I can spend the rest of the season thinking about whether to stay in the game or try on a new uniform.

He smiles. "I won't if you don't call me Robert." But he lets me off the hook. "My door is always open to you. So, tell me what you need."

X

"**M**an, I'm buzzing." Rickie is practically bouncing on the bench next to me at MacKay's. "I can't believe I got my first fucking NHL goal in my debut." We're surrounded by a lot of the team, celebrating a solid win over the Dallas Comets.

The kid glowed when he took his solo lap in warmups as the home crowd cheered for his introduction to the NHL. And he paid the fans back with some fantastic play. His TOI, or time on ice, was only a little over ten minutes, yet late in the third period, he made the most of his last shift of the game. We won a board battle in our O-Zone; the puck slipped to Karl Nilsson, who quickly passed it across ice to Ansel. He was wide open above the left dot and sniped the biscuit. The slapshot hit the top corner and into the net. Our fans went wild for the kid, and our players on the ice swarmed him in congratulations. When Sonny presented Rickie's goal puck in the locker room, the kid became speechless, wearing a face-splitting grin. It's a tradition in hockey to give the rookie their scoring puck, just like in other milestones, like a hundredth career goal.

Talk about glowing. Cat, Jenny, and another woman I don't recognize emerge from the parking lot. I'm biased, but my girl is the most beautiful fucking person I've ever seen. Especially now, when her eyes find me across the crowded patio, and she smiles. Operation Hide in Plain Sight is officially underway, although why Josh had to give it such a dramatic name, I'll never understand. Marketing guys are a little out there for me, and that's speaking as a goalie. Goalies are a known weird breed of players. As she approaches, Rickie takes a huge gulp of his beer, I'm guessing for courage, because he apologizes for crashing into me for the hundredth time.

"Thanks for understanding about me plowing into you. I can't believe that asshole got away with cross checking me in the first place and losing my edges to crash and burn into the net. You've been one of my heroes since I was a kid. I'm so embarrassed I did that. Normally, I'm not such a fucking loser."

Ouch. The reminder that I've been playing since this kid was in elementary school hurts more than the actual hit. Then Catherine's hand touches my shoulder, and I forget all about it.

"May I?" She points to the spot on the other side of me on the bench, the spot the guys made sure was vacant for her. I told them about her hanging out with us to protect her image, and they were all on board.

"Please," I stand and wait for her to take her seat out of habit. It's how I was raised, and I don't think about it looking suspicious until it's too late. But I glance around, and no one is taking pictures or posting that shit on Instagram. In a bar packed full of fans, no one even noticed. I smile, thinking this may be easier than we thought.

Jenny sits in Sonny's lap, but the stranger stands off to the side, looking star-struck. Cat nods at Ansel, who's still tripping over his apology, and leans in close. Not delivering the kiss I would have preferred, but baby steps. Instead, her lips brush my ear as if she has to lean in to be *heard*.

"What's all that about?"

I laugh and risk putting my hand on her thigh under the table, out of sight of prying eyes. "Weren't you watching the game? Ric got a little enthusiastic trying to strip the puck on his backcheck."

Bri snorts. "Enthusiastic? Hey, rook, do we need to go over how to stop at tomorrow's practice? First, you shave the ice, then you bend your knees and put your toes together like a snowplow."

The surrounding players howl in amusement. To his credit, Rickie turns beet red but laughs at himself, along with everyone else. Everybody knows about the failed penalty call.

When the kid got pushed at his speed, he was going down. Except Holt, of course, who shakes his head and mutters something about how low the AHL standards have sunk. Asshole.

"Congrats on a terrific game, Ansel, the first of many with the Quakes, I'm sure." Catherine gifts him one of her smiles, and my cock jumps in excitement. Or irritation that someone else is receiving her blessings, I'm not sure. I have to rein in my need to claim her as mine, or this little plan will never work. "Guys, I'd like to introduce you to Jennifer Jeske. She's the fan who won the Quakes' Experience by calling into the radio station contest and naming the most players within thirty seconds. Jennifer, meet Zach—"

"Oh, I know who all the players are. I'm such a big fan, I even named my son Jason." We all stare at her for a moment, which makes her visibly uncomfortable. "After Jason Toll?"

We break out in a combination of relief and honest-to-God laughter. "Sorry," Luka explains, "I didn't know who you were talking about for a minute. I don't think I've ever heard anyone call Tolli 'Jason' the two years I played with him." It might have sounded like he was making fun of her, but between the accent and the killer smile, she laughs along with us.

"Thank God, I was worried you were staring at me because you thought I was nuts."

The guys make a place for our Super Fan at the table and start regaling her with stories about Tolli and some of the other past greats.

"Remember the epic goal he made in game five of the playoffs? Tolli got tripped, landed on his ass, and still took his shot anyway," Luka reminisces.

"The trip ended up being lucky because the goalie had been set, and with Toll's fall and shooting while sliding on his ass across the ice, the puck completely slipped past the blocker," Brian adds.

"Plus"—Zach lifts a finger—"the power play we got from that tripping penalty was the nail in the lid to New Jersey's coffin."

We may not like talking about ourselves much, but there's nothing a hockey player loves more than telling hockey stories about somebody else. The guys surrounding Jennifer continue to regale her with Stanley Cup stories.

"Hey," Cat says into my ear, my skin tingling where her lips brush against it. "You ready to get out of here?"

I love my guys, but I've wanted to have my hands on her bare skin since she crossed the patio. I know she's only been here for twenty minutes or so, but fuck it. "Hell yeah," I reply, leaning in to nuzzle her neck but keeping enough distance so it looks like two people trying to talk in a large, noisy crowd.

"Meet me in the parking lot in five." Then, loud enough for everyone to hear, she announces, "I'm going to the ladies' room. I'll be right back." With a wink in my direction, she heads into the brewery toward the restrooms. She'll cross through the large warehouse and exit on the opposite side, getting lost in the crowd. It makes me laugh seeing her try to be sneaky. Bri snickers from across the table.

"Super slick," he jokes and then nods toward the parking lot, wordlessly encouraging me to get the hell out of Dodge. I empty my beer in one swallow, excuse myself on the pretext of going to get another at the bar, and disappear into the crowd on the patio before any asshole asks me to bring them back another too.

I'm heading to my car when I hear a *psst* from a dark corner of the parking lot. I look around, and since Catherine is nowhere to be found, I'm banking it's her and not a seductive mugger. Swiveling my head again to make sure no one is watching, I go to where a busted light has granted us a murky cover from prying eyes. I can barely make out Cat's form before she grabs my jacket and pulls me in for a deep kiss.

"This isn't exactly private," I murmur into her mouth.

"The thrill of getting caught makes it even sexier," she moans as I reach a hand under her blank team sweater bearing no name or number and touch her warm skin. Can't be seen as being partial to any one player now, can she? But one day, I hope she wears number thirty-three in public. For the time being, I get the precious view privately in my bedroom and around my house. I love it when she wears my jersey and nothing else. "Were you limping just now?"

My dick deflates with an almost audible wheeze. Nothing throws cold water on a libido like being reminded you're fucking old. "A little." Because I won't lie to Catherine, I may downplay something, but I won't outright hide the truth.

"From where that idiot kept hitting you with his stick to get the puck you clearly covered?" she growls. "It should have been goalie interference. I'm proud of Holt jumping him and kicking his ass."

"Ooh, I love it when you talk hockey and get all chirpy." I attempt to get us back on track to making out against whoever's SUV we're leaning on. Although if it's Trev's, odds are this isn't the first time the outside has seen action. Definitely wouldn't want to turn a black light on the inside. It would look like a Pollock painting. She meets my attempts to get back to business with a smack on my hand.

"Let's go to your place so I can see the damage in proper light." She stalks off, leaving me to pull myself together as she heads to my car. "Part of the Super Fan experience was a private party limo to and from the game, so I don't have my car."

"You can damage a guy by giving him blue balls like this," I call out to her retreating back. Her only answer is a burst of very unsympathetic laughter. So much for my James Bond act. Obediently, I catch up to her as fast as my leg will allow and unlock my car for her.

X

"Wow," Cat murmurs as she traces the black, purple, and green bruise across my ribs, just below my armpit from where Ricar's shoulder forcibly slid into me. "The kid's lucky he's on our side. If someone from the Comets had done that, the entire team would have piled on and beaten the shit out of him for hitting the goalie like they did earlier for you." She presses a little harder on the darkest spot on the word "hitting," eliciting a hiss of pain from me. "Oh, does that hurt? Maybe you should have been icing that instead of drinking beers at MacKay's."

We barely passed through my door before she stripped my suit jacket and shirt off. I kicked it closed with expectations of more sensual pleasure until she saw the bruise and switched from sexy spy to nurse. I mean, it's Cat, so it's all sexy, but I'm not happy with the direction this is going. It's not like she hasn't seen me banged up after a game. It comes with the territory of stopping ninety-mile-per-hour pucks. Luckily, my pants are still on, so she hasn't seen my thigh yet. That injury the team retaliated for.

In the second period, I'd stopped a shot from the new guy on the Comets. Some Swedish player whose name escapes me, but for me, will forevermore be the Fucking Swede because he just couldn't deal with the fact I'd covered the puck. The asshole whaled away on me with his stick, and I have no idea why the ref didn't blow the whistle, stopping play. A couple of tries to dig the puck out from my hold, I get, but this went on for what seemed an eternity. He wasn't even aiming for my glove, just pounding on my exposed thigh. My legs were in the lower butterfly position, so my leg blockers were popped off my quads.

I was getting ready to punch the guy myself but couldn't get my blocker off while keeping the puck covered. Then I saw gloves and a stick hit the ice. I glanced up and saw Holt grab the other player by the sweater, a huge shit-eating grin on his face. He yanked him away from the net, although not far enough away for my taste. The razor-sharp blades were a little too close for comfort, but he was swinging away like a prizefighter, and it's tough to control where your feet go on the ice. Hearing Holt chirp and swear, "Get the fuck away from my goalie," it was almost as if we were friends. Almost. In moments, the rest of the team joined the melee, half of them fighting and the other half trying to break things up. I'm not sure which half Rickie was on, but his first fight and his first goal in the same game? He was two-thirds of the way to a Gordie Howe hat trick.

"It was the kid's first NHL game. I couldn't miss the cellie because of a minor bruise."

She rolls her eyes, but from the upward kick at the corner of her mouth, I know she gets it. Until her brow furrows in concern. "Are you playing Saturday?"

"Thank Christ, no," I say, and for once, truly relieved not to be on the ice in the next game. "Raki's in the net." Tomorrow is a travel day, and then we play the Montreal Royals.

She reaches for my belt buckle. I grab her neck and pull her in for a kiss, hoping to distract her, but she's having none of it. "Linc, although the bruise on your upper body is spectacular, you're not limping because of it."

Dammit. When crossing the parking lot, I was so eager to get my hands on her I forgot to mask my limp. With a sigh, I let her have her way. I kick off my shoes, and after that, Catherine takes over. She makes quick work of unbuckling my belt, followed by the button and zipper. With a slight push, my slacks fall to the ground. I'm more than a little aroused by having her take charge and strip me so efficiently. I could learn to love this.

"What the hell?" I grimace as she drops to her knees right in front of me. While she's examining my thigh, my cock has other ideas about the proximity of those lips. She'll just have to deal with the way it's standing at attention for her. By now, she must know what's going to happen if she stays in that position.

"Linc, how are you even walking?" Her cool fingers lightly stroke my thigh, which is not helping with my other problem at the moment. I'm so turned on I ache, and it's not from the bruising.

"I'm fine." I reach down and pull her to her feet. "It looks worse than it feels." The contusion covers a large portion of my left quadriceps, and I'm lying. It's sore as hell, and I dread when the rule of forty-eight hours sets in. The team doc did what he could for it during the intermission, and moving around in the third was better for the bruise than sitting on the bench. Hopefully, he'll work his miracles on the injury before we have to leave to catch the plane.

"Come on." She grabs my hand, drags me to my couch, and pushes me down. Obviously, I let her because there'd be no way she could manhandle me if I didn't want her to. She may be on the tall side for a woman, but I outmuscle her. "I'm going to get the ice, and then I'm off to find your arnica gel and ibuprofen." Giving me a glaring once over, she ignores the erection tenting my boxers.

Catherine is true to her word. I'm icing my ribs and thigh as she struts down to my bedroom. She takes longer than expected. After all, she knows where I keep my medical supplies. It's not her first rodeo. I figure out the reason the moment she leaves my bedroom.

She sashays down the hallway wearing only my jersey, which reaches mid-thigh on her. At least, I assume she's naked beneath because she knows what I love. And sure enough, she also holds the gel and painkillers. She places her supplies on the coffee table before sitting on the couch. Snuggling into my good side—because the bruises are both on my left—I wrap an arm around her.

I pull her leg over my right so she's lying more on top of

him, rushing blood heating my cheeks. Mom was right. As sexy as I feel in this dress, if I had seen Linc, I might have done something completely inappropriate.

"Honey, we're so happy you told us. It's not like I didn't have an inkling from the way you've been floating around the office, but it was nice to hear it from your own lips."

A terrifying thought makes me grip the stem of my wineglass so tight it might shatter. "Has this been affecting my work?"

His deep chuckle rumbles. "On the contrary, I think having something more than just the idea of a team to care about has made you more ruthless. I think even Carter was a little afraid of you once or twice during the trade meetings."

"Yeah, but if it's so obvious, maybe this is a bad idea. Should I stay away from him and leave early?" I was really looking forward to tonight, figuring Linc and I would be able to share at least one dance in public as long as I dance with some of the other players, too.

"Nonsense, we've got you covered. We invited players to join us at the Bishop table for dinner, which is totally normal for this shindig." He winks. "Of course, being the family table, that means Daniel will be there, but that can't be helped. Ever since Shannon left him, he's been like a thorny cactus."

I refrain from pointing out that my brother is a douche, not just because of his crumbling marriage. My parents know I haven't told him about my relationship yet. I used the excuse of his divorce and not wanting to make him feel worse, though it's hard not to spill everything to my father about my brother's plans to screw me out of my team. He doesn't need the added stress. Speaking of issues, poor Linc. It's going to be a trial by fire for him to sit with Daniel. Hopefully, at least, they will be seated on far opposite sides.

We are the last to reach the large circular table. Everyone smiles at me except Daniel, of course. Mom and Josh are elegance of the evening. Thank God we aren't the New York Marauders with their hideous orange and blue color scheme.

The black-tie affair raises money for a different charity each year. The entrance fee, by table or plate, is hefty, assuring the generous donors an evening of good food, dancing, and, of course, the chance to rub elbows with the team, who are required to attend. The biggest moneymaker of the night is the silent auction, which is always filled with amazing items. Most are hockey-related, like a sweater signed by the whole team or a game-winning puck, but some aren't. Stays at vacation homes and helicopter tours of Catalina are popular, courtesy of the corporations sponsoring entire tables.

My long-sleeved, copper-colored Vera Wang sheath gown hugs my body. Its high slit makes walking easy. Add in the low dip in the back, baring my skin, and the dress is sexy yet tasteful. I can't wait for Linc to see me. Speaking of which, I scan the large, crowded event space, seeking him out. Normally, he'd be easy to locate since he's so tall, but the room is filled with tall, hulking hockey players dressed in high-end suits or tuxes. I don't spot him, but my father finds me.

He approaches and kisses my cheek. "You look beautiful."

"Thanks, you're rather snazzy yourself." And I mean it. At sixty-five, he still looks dashing in his classic navy Dior tuxedo, custom-tailored to fit his broad but trim frame. His dark hair, with a dash of gray sprinkled through it, is brushed back with care, as opposed to its normal mussy state. He holds out his arm, which I wrap my own around as he escorts me to the bar so we can enjoy a quick cocktail before taking our seats for dinner.

"I know, not the escort you're looking for, but your mother told me to come over and grab you before Linc sees you in that dress and blows your cover story," he informs me, a delighted smile lighting his eyes.

"Dad, you'll always be my number one man," I assure

CHAPTER
Sixteen

CATHERINE

I step into the Grand Parisian Ballroom at the prestigious Mayfair Hotel, where the Quakes' Foundation's annual gala and silent auction is taking place this year. It looks like I've been transported to a baronial hall of a European castle. The delicate crystal chandeliers offset heavy exposed wood beams in the ceiling. The French Aubusson carpet is an elegant, muted pattern before giving way to a dance floor, and the tall stained glass windows are framed by rich but tasteful drapes. I'm honestly not into home decor, so the best I can say is the material swoops over the arched casements and cascades down the sides. The mirrors in the curved wall niches reflect the light so you can see the people across the table from you, but it's warmer than the glare of most modern hotel ballrooms. There's even a balcony for the musicians to sit above the din of the guests. But in our case, the space holds the DJ's equipment.

Tonight, the place is decorated in the Quakes' colors of black and white with silver accents, only adding to the me. If I have to endure the fucking freezing ice, I'm using her as a blanket.

"Has it been twenty minutes yet?"

"Don't be a baby. You still have fifteen to go."

I kiss the top of her head, her silky hair brushing against my lips. "Thanks for taking care of me."

She snuggles in closer. "Thanks for letting me. Now, how shall we pass the next fifteen minutes until it's time to take the ice off?" A sly smile lights her face.

It's a little tricky, but we find a way for some fun.

there. Zach, his wife Jenny, Luka with a gorgeous date, and there's Brian and Linc, who both came dateless. One for obvious reasons and the other as camouflage. No one wanted Linc to appear out of play by being the only one flying solo.

My dad pulls out my chair for me. It just so happens my secret boyfriend is sitting on my left while my father sits on my right.

"You look beautiful, Catherine." Brian compliments me from the other side of Linc with a mischievous glint in his eyes, especially when Linc stiffens in his seat. He said the words Linc wanted to say but couldn't. Sometimes, I don't get the teasing and taunting between the four of them, but I've hung out with the guys enough to know they constantly harass each other.

"Thank you." I brush my hand against Linc's under the table. "I have to admit, all the players have quite the dashing air about them tonight." I smile around the table before letting my gaze catch Linc's.

"Some of them," Jenny adjusts Zach's permanently crooked blood-red bow tie, "take more work than others." She casts an overly dramatic, dreamy gaze at the effortlessly handsome Luka.

"And some just wake up that way." Her husband responds with a guttural growl, and we all laugh as she kisses him on the cheek to prove she only has eyes for him.

"You wouldn't believe how hard it is to find a tuxedo in a hockey player's size," she adds with a smirk. We all know that the athletes have to go custom, nothing off the rack fits.

"We tried to bribe the tailor to put a big 'C' on Sonny's tux to make him feel more comfortable," Brian teases his fidgety captain. "Dude refused to do it." Everyone at the table, except for Daniel, of course, laughs. Luka's date, a model gorgeous young woman with huge brown eyes, looks confused and seems to laugh along with the majority to fit in.

"Your efforts paid off on both of your behalfs." I smile at

Jenny, whose hair and makeup perfectly sync with her chic, regal gown in the same shade of red as her husband's tie.

"Nothing like spending three hours at a salon. It was fun at first, but by the end, I was starting to feel bad for movie stars who have to dress up all the time." Again, the table chuckles, except for Luka's date.

Ever the hostess, my mother must have noticed the young woman's slight disconnect too and tries to pull her into the conversation. "I'm sorry, I don't think we've met," she says, giving her a warm smile. "I'm Amahle, and this is my husband, Robert."

The woman stares blankly at her and then to Luka, who says something to her in a language I think is Italian. She responds with a sexy string of sounds and a passionate kiss.

A hand slides up my left thigh, and my body reacts. Linc and I have been together for almost three months, but it's been only the last three weeks since we started this game of being together secretly yet out in the open, and I'm insanely jealous of Luka and his date right now.

"This is Sophia Giordano. She doesn't speak English."

"How…interesting," my mother replies with a slight arch of her brow. "Please, tell her she's very welcome here." Whatever that translation is, it ends with more smooching. Clearly, *they* speak the same language.

Conversation comes to a halt as the first course arrives, and the head of the Foundation steps to the microphone. Maureen McGuire has raised thousands of dollars for our charity. She wanted to retire this season, but my dad somehow talked her into one more year.

"Thank you all for attending and all the money you'll be spending tonight." The room fills with chuckles. "The silent auction is officially open, and the dancing will start in about an hour. So, please enjoy your meal, and on behalf of Quakes' Aid, thank you for your continued support and generosity." She receives applause as she steps away.

Linc's large hand grasps my thigh, and he joins the conversation. "Did everyone catch Luka's *Inside Look* on the Quakes' YouTube channel? Have you seen how many hits it has?"

Luka smirks. "I've surpassed our dear captain." His video must have displaced Zach's player profile from the number-one spot since it aired last season.

Zach doesn't seem upset by this at all. The Quakes, like any NHL team, have a bunch of videos on their channels. We have behind-the-scenes like *Inside Look*, highlight reels, goofy stuff, and all kinds of things to engage the fan base.

"I'd lay money," Josh adds, "the percentage of viewership skews female, and their panties have spontaneously melted worldwide. However, he's probably melted more than a few men's boxers as well." The table explodes in laughter. Josh should know since he's head of marketing, but all you have to do is look at Luka Ribic to know the truth.

He's beyond classically handsome. His whiskey-colored eyes are the first to draw you in, always filled with mischief and daring, with a promise to do dirty things to you. His dark brown hair is thick and stylish, begging you to run your fingers through the plush locks to help with the artfully mussed appearance. His beard and mustache are the perfectly controlled scruffy five o'clock shadow highlighting his masculine square jaw and full lips. Classic sharp cheekbones frame his long, straight, unbroken nose—almost impossible to achieve in professional hockey. In short, Luka is more than model-ready. And since I've gotten to know him now, I've realized he's more than just one of the best left wingers in the league. He's smart, funny, and an incredible guy. But no matter how drool worthy he is, Lincoln is the only man who heats my blood.

My dad clears his throat, obviously about to change the topic to something less risqué than our left winger's ability to make women have sex with him. "So, gentlemen, how is our newest addition fitting in?" We traded a couple of Tsunami players and a draft pick for a veteran left-shot D-Man, Alex Bouchard, to help us in the push to the playoffs.

"He's fitting right in with Z. It's kind of scary how well." Zach acknowledges. Z is Anzor Zaytseva. He's on the second line as the right-handed defenseman, who also happens to be our oldest player at thirty-eight. He's still playing at the top of his game—age hasn't slowed him down at all. "No doubt he'll help us to the first seed in the Pacific in record time."

"What about Rickie? How'd he take getting sent back to the Tsunami?" Luka asks. "Some guys don't deal with it so well."

"He knew the move to the NHL was temporary when he was promoted. He's happy Rue healed so quickly." Linc clarified. "I talked to him the other day, and he was jazzed about how he can help raise the game for some of his teammates from what he learned. I think we put him through development camp in the summer, and he'll be one of our strongest rooks for next season."

The table erupts in the guys and gals excitedly talking over each other at the mentions of summer and development camp. The players all take advantage of the time off after the playoffs, but they all keep in the know about what goes on. Brian gives Linc a look and mouths, "We?" with a smirk.

"Gentlemen," my mother interrupts, shooting Dad a pointed glare. "This is your night off, so why don't you leave business back at the office, or rink, as it were, and talk about something else? What are you all looking to bid for at the silent auction?"

That's weird. Mom usually loves talking about the game almost as much as Dad and I do. Then I follow her gaze and see Daniel accept another whiskey from the server. The way he tilts the alcohol on the way to his mouth, sloshing some out before he can belt it back, is clear evidence this isn't his first.

"Yeah, 'cause talking about what puck you're going to bid on is so much more interesting than going on and on about who's going to be the next superstar," he mutters. I'm not even sure he realizes he said that part out loud.

An uncomfortable silence hangs over the table as the dinner dishes are replaced by dessert. It's an amazing black and white mousse in our team's colors, but everyone seems to have the same lack of appetite that I'm experiencing. *What the hell is going on with Daniel?*

"There is that two-week stay at the Baoase Luxury Resort in Curaçao I have my eye on," Luka says, with a lascivious look at his date. We all laugh, knowing it's unlikely he'll still be with her by the time the summer break comes. If he wins the bid, he won't have any problems finding someone to accompany him.

The last of the plates are being cleared, and second cups of coffee are poured for those interested. The DJ starts the music, playing a Frank Sinatra classic, while people begin mingling at the bar, yet no one steps on the dance floor. My mom, the experienced hostess that she is, takes my dad's hand. "Come on, Fred Astaire, let's show these kids how it's done." Their appearance is apparently what everyone is waiting for because as soon as they start dancing, a half-dozen other couples join them. Linc squeezes my thigh under the table but pretends to watch my parents rather than meeting my gaze. I sneak a peek at Daniel and catch him watching me expectantly. *Shit.* No chance of dancing with my guy while eagle eyes is watching.

"Excuse me, pretty lady, but may I have this dance?" Brian stands and offers me his hand. There's an amused twinkle in his eyes, but I'm not sure if it's because of Linc or Daniel. Either way, screw it. If Josh's plan of hiding my very close relationship with Linc behind the smokescreen of hanging out with the team is going to work, I might as well enjoy myself.

"It would be my pleasure." I take his hand and let him

lead me to the dance floor. Glancing over my shoulder, I see Linc roll his eyes, the corner of his mouth curling upward in a crooked smile, while Daniel grabs another drink. With any luck, he'll pass out soon, and I can quietly dance the night away in the arms of my guy. Mostly.

From years of watching him on the ice, I'm not surprised that our highest-scoring player is confident and graceful on the dance floor. He also smells great. Like all the players, he's taller than me, so putting my hand on his broad shoulder is a reach, but it feels nice. I gaze into his hazel eyes, curtained by those thick, long lashes that come naturally to some men, and say the first dumb thing that comes to my mind or out of my mouth.

"Why hasn't some lucky woman snapped you up already?" I really have gotten to know Brian, Luka, and Sonny with all the hanging out we've been doing. They are all terrific guys. Jenny was smart to nail Zach down when she did.

Fortunately, he takes no offense and laughs it off. "Did my mom set you up to ask that?" He shakes his head and twirls me in an elegant move. "I'm not relationship material yet, but one day. Besides, my sister, Phoebe, is moving to town and will be staying with me until she finds a place of her own. I feel my cock being blocked already."

I can't stop the laugh which escapes me. "If you change your mind, let me know. You might be the man to tame my friend Brittany."

"Like you did our Caveman?" Just as he says this, the music changes to a smooth foxtrot. Harry Connick Jr's velvet voice sings *It Had To Be You*. He flawlessly leads me into that as well. There's graceful, and then there's a well-schooled dancer. At my arched eyebrow, he sighs. "Year before last, I took dance lessons to get ready for my sister's wedding. I had to play the role of father of the bride and didn't want to be a big dumb oaf when we did the obligatory dance." He smirks.

"Turns out all the lessons weren't necessary after she caught her fiance cheating."

"Oh no. Is she okay?"

"Yeah, it's one of the reasons for the scenery change. The past year was rough, always running into that bastard."

I can sense him getting riled by the growl in his voice, so a change in conversation is necessary. "Do you attack everything like you're training for a game?" I smile, acknowledging his dancing skills. He really is very good. "And I think Linc is far from tamed."

"Seriously, I've known him for twelve years. And this is the happiest I've seen him in a long time. None of us thought we'd see him in a committed relationship after that Rainbow Raine disaster."

Ah yes, the infamous puck bunny who was splashed all over social media for her ten seconds of fame when she seduced Linc, waited until he got drunk celebrating winning the Cup, and married him in Las Vegas, of all places. Super classy. Naturally, the marriage didn't last long. I can't say I was disappointed when I heard the news they'd divorced almost as fast as they'd gotten together. Truth be told, I celebrated with Brittany and a couple of other college friends.

"Where was the team brotherhood that night? You couldn't have locked him in a closet until he sobered up?" I tease him.

He grimaces, playing along. "I might have been just a little drunk myself, but you know Linc. When he gets an idea in his head, there's no talking him out of it. Anyway, I want to say thanks. You've made him a happy man."

"And upped his game?" I joke. The theory currently circulating is that Linc is either getting a lot of sex or taking steroids, and since the players are tested regularly for any drugs, it's obvious that's not it.

"Sure, that's nice too, but I'm glad to see my friend so happy."

The music changes, and we break apart in time for me to take Linc's hand as he stops next to us. A quick glance over my shoulder, I spot the empty Bishop table.

"Don't worry. Josh took him to the coffee shop in the lobby to try to sober him up."

Relief floods me, and I happily step into his arms as we sway slowly to *Who We Love* while being serenaded by Sam Smith and Ed Sheeran. "I love you," he whispers.

"Love you, too," I answer as quietly. "I so want to kiss you right now."

"It's crossed my mind a thousand times tonight." He smiles down at me. "You realize you're killing me in that dress, right?" His warm hand slides lower, landing on the small of my back. My skin breaks out in goosebumps, his palm warm against my bare skin as he presses me closer to his large body. He's so handsome tonight in his custom tux.

"Right back at you. You are so hot in a tuxedo."

"I want to press my lips over yours. Nibble on your lower lip, teasing you open." A shudder chases through me at his low, rough words. "I'd slip my tongue inside and taste you. Tonight, you'll be flavored with chocolate mousse, champagne, and you. I'll never get enough of tasting your mouth, your delicious satiny skin. You're my new addiction."

"Linc." His name comes out a whine. He knows how his dirty talk gets to me, and it's too early to try to sneak out. He's a freaking tease. Linc chuckles, proving me correct. He knows exactly what he's doing.

A loud slap startles me in his arms, drawing my attention to an attractive woman. She storms off from Matthew Holt, whose hand is pressed to his cheek, but doesn't hide his ugly sneer thrown at her departing back. I've been watching him. The happier the family vibe at a party, the more of an asshole he becomes. I turn away and sigh.

Linc squeezes me in a quick hug as we sway. "Don't let him get to you. It's over, and he hasn't ruined the event."

"I'm worried about him. He wasn't always an angry bastard. His last two teams had only great things to say about him personally."

"What do you think changed? All I've seen is the wall he's built between the team and himself." Linc's lips compress into a thin line. "I mean, last season, his play was actually dangerous on the ice, but it's better now. I'll give him that."

"Yeah, last season was rough. The Quakes had no idea what he was going through. Had I known, I would have pushed the trade deal aside and waited to go after him later, even if he couldn't have participated in the playoffs."

"What are you talking about?" He frowns.

"His sister was dying. The Pittsburg Emperors kept quiet and traded him when she only had weeks to live."

"Holy shit. I had no idea. Was that why he disappeared in the middle of March?"

"He begged my dad for time off. That's when Matt learned we didn't know about his sister." Linc brushes his thumb over my wrist with his hand holding mine. "My dad was livid at Pittsburg's deception and apologized on behalf of our organization. He let Matt go immediately, but it was too late. She died before he could get there."

"Well, fuck. Now, I can understand his behavior. He probably hates the NHL, especially the way the Emperors treated him. No wonder he doesn't want to get close to us with such a betrayal under his belt. Just fuck."

I so wanted to press my head to his chest and tuck myself into his strong arms. It's horrible what Matt went through. He's so guarded and angry, and who could blame him?

CHAPTER
Seventeen

LINCOLN

"Oh my God, I did it! I got a hole-in-one!"

I laugh at Cat's antics as she dances around the crazy giant clown head on the miniature golf course, making that "in-your-face" move to Zach, Jenny, Luka, and his current flavor of the month. Don't get me wrong, he's not as much of a manwhore as Trevor, but he keeps a steady rotation. The funny thing is, even when they go their separate ways, he leaves them smiling. When Cat flaunts her victory in my face, the heat that flickers in her eyes says there's something else she'd rather put my face into, but that will have to wait.

After we play a round and grab some food at MacKay's, we'll leave separately and meet at my place. Then we'll start with my face buried deep between her legs, licking her incredible taste, and move on from there. For now, I pull her behind the windmill on the hole next to us and give her a fast, hard kiss when no one's looking.

I fully support her dream and know that when she's

named the first female owner of an NHL team, our relationship is going to have to change. Thank fuck that hasn't happened yet, though. It's been a month since Operation Hide in Plain Sight was launched, thanks to help from my boys and Josh. It's hard to believe it's April already. The end of the regular season is only a few games away. We manage to sneak off two or three nights a week, depending on our game schedule. I wish she could come on the road with us, but even though we aren't Ryan Reynolds and Blake Lively famous, the time she tried it nearly ended in disaster.

We were playing the Fishers a couple of weeks back. Because of the distance to Vancouver, the timing of the game, and the fact we had two days before the next game, the team spent two nights in Vancouver. I had no idea she was planning on doing this, but when we took to the ice to warm up, there was Catherine and her dad on the JumboTron, chatting with the owner of the Fishers in his box. And that turned into an embarrassing moment as I tripped and face-planted on the ice.

Fortunately, things improved after that. Out of twenty-two shots on goal, I let exactly zero get in. I don't want to even think the 'S' word for fear of jinxing myself, but needless to say, I was pretty stoked after the game. Excitement turned into a gut-churning need when I got a text from Cat instructing me to meet her outside the hotel in ten minutes. The thought was for us to sneak out and grab a drink, but we weren't counting on the intensity of Canadian hockey fans, even for the opposing team. In moments, they swarmed me, but luckily, no one recognized her.

Not wanting the exposure, we headed back to the hotel. When we reached the Quakes' floor, Foursie, Mikey, and Clutch spotted us. Catherine kept walking, right past my door and all the way down the hall to her own room, alone. If we ever try again, I may spring for a private room off the team's floor. She was pretty shaken, so I'm not holding my breath.

"Hey, Jon Rahm, it's your turn to shoot," Jenny calls to Catherine. The way she and Zach so casually have their arms looped around one another makes me burn with jealousy more than Luka's dating pool does.

While Luka explains the golf champ's reference to his date, a very smart librarian type who, oddly enough, knows nothing about sports, including hockey, Cat goes over to the next hole on the course. She scrunches her face in an adorable, thoughtful pout at the dragon whose mouth keeps opening and closing for the direct way while its wings flap the possible side routes. "How am I supposed to play that?"

Not being the big dumb jock everyone assumes hockey players are, I mosey over to "help" her. "Here, I'll show you." Her ball is already on the center tee, so I place my hands on her hips, nudging her into position. "Now, line up your shot." Here comes the fun part as I curve myself around her, my legs outside hers as my chin rests on her shoulder, and I wrap my hands over hers, grasping the club. The minx pushes her ass against my cock, which, rightly so, shows his appreciation. "Keep your eye on the mouth," I whisper into her ear and feel her shiver. Hoping my timing is correct, I use my hold over hers and pull back the club. It taps the ball, which heads in a straight line right toward the gaping mouth.

Reluctantly, I pull away and straighten as we watch the ball. It hits the closed mouth, travels down the side shoot, and collides with a wing. The ball shoots backward and travels all the way to the tee. *Score*! I burst out laughing. I couldn't have made her whiff it any worse. She spins to me with a glare.

"You did that on purpose!" I can't stop laughing, and now everyone else joins in. "I can't believe you did that."

"Can you blame me? You are kicking our collective asses. I had to do something." Just like almost every hockey player knows how to golf, Catherine learned at her dad's side. Her skill on eighteen holes seems to have transferred to the putt-putt course.

She smirks and then tees up. She taps the ball. It goes straight, right down the dragon's throat. We both rush to the backside and watch the ball drop into the hole. "Ha! That's only two strokes. Choke on that, Mister Cheater."

I grab her and kiss her. "Who knew you were so competitive?" I take her hand and lead her to the front, where Zach is lining up his shot.

He smiles as we approach, glancing at our clasped hands. "It went in, didn't it?"

"Yup." I give a chin lift. "My woman kicks ass."

A phone rings, and it must be Catherine's because she drops my hand and reaches into her back pocket to grab her cell. "It's my mom's ringtone." She steps off to the side. I keep one eye on her and the other on the play.

"What? No!" She turns deathly pale and reaches a hand out to brace on a tree as if to keep herself from falling. I'm instantly at her side, wrapping my arm around her shoulder. Tears are streaming down her face. "Which hospital?" She listens to her mom's response. "I'll get there as soon as possible."

Everyone is surrounding her, all with concerned expressions. She's trembling in my hold. "What's happened? Talk to me, Cat."

"My-my d-dad," she stutters. "He's had a heart attack. They're taking him in for surgery."

Oh fuck. This is bad. "What hospital?"

"C-Cedar Sinai."

I glance at Zach. "On it," he pulls out his phone. He'll get a hold of Coach, who will spread the news to the team.

Leading Catherine to the exit, I don't think she knows she's crying, but that's the least of our concerns. I want to tell her everything will be all right, but I can't. Shit happens. All I can do is pray, look after her, and be her strength. We reach her car, and the doors are unlocked from the proximity of her keys. I help her into the passenger seat and buckle her in. She robotically hands me her key fob. Her hand brushes mine, and they're icy cold.

I hop into the driver's side, push the seat all the way back, and press the ignition. After turning the heater to high and hitting the passenger-side seat warmer, I back out of the parking spot. My job is to get her to her mom safely and hope for the best.

X

As a hockey player, I've seen the inside of many hospitals. Sometimes, as the patient in the ER, sometimes bringing in a teammate or friend who broke, split, or tore something on the ice. Two years ago, I was a patient in this very hospital when I had surgery to fix my labral tear, so I know it all too well. Waiting rooms are never the way they're depicted on TV. They aren't bright and spacious, with a television quietly playing in the background and a hushed ambiance as a few family members and friends wait to hear about a patient. The reality is the waiting room isn't where a hospital focuses its resources. They are small, uncomfortable, and crowded with multiple families waiting to find out about the fate of their loved one, suspiciously glancing at each other as if the survival of one reduces the odds of the other patients. Even with the Bishop's level of money, the first half-hour plays out exactly the same. However, because of the team and the notoriety of the players, we eventually score a private waiting room. So it's only family, so to speak.

It's all I can do not to punch the bland, white wall, that's how much it physically hurts to see Cat in so much pain as we wait for news about her father. We've been here for several hours, enough time for Bri, Mikey, Coach O'Ryan, and some of the Quakes' staff members to join us, with more trickling in every minute. Even Holt is here, huddled off in a corner by himself. After what Catherine told me about his sister, I know this has got to be hard for him, but that's the Quakes for you. As much as Robert Bishop always treats us like family, we look up to him. At this rate, as teammates and staff continue to pour in, we're going to overflow the private area and spill into the hallway.

Cat oscillates between hugging her mother, who is taking this ordeal with regal grace, and pacing the room, hands clasping and unclasping repeatedly, though maneuvering is getting tight because of all the large men filling the space. She and Josh have an unspoken tag team arrangement, with him sitting by their mother's side when she paces and vice versa. Daniel, who looked pretty ragged when he got here, sits off alone, shaking off any gesture of comfort from his siblings. Frankly, after what Cat told me about him, I couldn't give two shits about the guy. He doesn't deserve a father like Robert Bishop, but no one ever said life was fair. Much as I wanted to beat the shit out of him for the pressure he's putting on Catherine to walk away from her dream, all I can focus on right now is making sure she's okay, and I didn't care who sees it.

I nod to Bri, who leaves for a moment and comes back with a few bottles of water. I take one and stop Cat on her thousandth lap past me while he gives the others to Josh and Mrs. Khoza-Bishop. Out of the corner of my eye, I see them accept the offering numbly as if they're not even sure what it is. Cat shakes her head, refusing to take it.

"Cat, just drink a little, you need to—"

Before I can finish, she yanks the plastic bottle out of my hands and throws it against the wall. "I don't understand this. Dad exercises every day, he watches what he eats, he-he…" She trembles, fighting the tears, but dammit, they always win. I do the only thing I can and take her in my arms, having no fucks left to give anymore about who sees us. The only thing that matters is easing her pain in any way I can. The sobs racking her body tear my heart out. Daniel makes an ugly, disapproving sound, and I reconsider my promise not to kill him.

Her sobs subside, so I lead her to a couple of chairs the boys clear out for us. I can't lie to her and say her dad will be fine—he might not. But I have to offer her something, so I go with the only thing I know to be true. "I'm here for you, baby, I've got you."

Time drags by. Raki and Eddie are mumbling, each in their own language. I look over and see they're both holding rosaries and reciting prayers. It's not my thing, being raised Protestant and not very devout at that, but I respect their faith. Any little bit to tip the scale in Robert's direction will help.

Finally, after what feels like an eternity, a woman wearing surgical scrubs and an exhausted expression comes into the waiting room. At the sight of all the burly hockey players, she pauses for a moment, eyes going wide. Her gaze settles on Amahle, and she strides confidently over to her. Based on her body language, I'm betting on good news, but Cat's grasp on my hand tightens. Maybe she's not so sure or doesn't dare to hope. I wrap my arm around her shoulders and give her a gentle squeeze.

"Mrs. Bishop?" Catherine's mother stands, not correcting her name, chin raised, meeting whatever the news might be with incredible poise. Taking her standing as an acknowledgment that she's got the right person, the doctor continues. "I'm Doctor Jones. We met earlier when your husband came into the emergency room."

"Yes, I remember." The woman is showing more strength than I would. I'd have shaken the surgeon, demanding to cut the bullshit and tell me if he's alive or not. But she pauses for a deep breath, and I realize she's gathering all the calm she

can manage before hearing the next few words that could change her life forever. "How did the surgery go?" The doctor looks around at all of us like she's worried about giving out privileged information with so many of us around. "It's okay, Dr. Jones. We're all family here."

"I'm happy to report your husband came through with flying colors. There were a few blockages, but they weren't as bad as we'd initially suspected, so a simple coronary angioplasty was sufficient. We had to insert two stents." The collective sigh of relief from almost twenty giant human beings, as well as the family and staff, startles the doctor for a moment before she continues. "He'll need to take it easy for a while but should make a full recovery. You'll need to set a schedule with a physical therapist, but we can take care of that later. He's in recovery right now, but as soon as we move him to a room, a nurse will come and escort you." She glances around and nails us all with a laser stare. "And only you can visit for a few minutes."

It's a good thing we were still sitting because Cat sags with relief into my arms like all the tension, as well as her strength, has rushed out of her body. Much as I love having her in my arms for all the world to see, there's one place she needs to be more, and that's with her mother and brothers. I help her to her feet and guide her over so she, her mom, and Josh tearfully cling to each other, palpably relieved at the outcome.

That fucker Daniel puts a hand on his mother's back, but the look on his face is anything but relief. He looks like he got the news that the old man had died rather than that he's going to be okay. What is with that scowl? Some people.

I get the feeling his fuckery has only just started. That he thinks his father's heart attack has opened the door for his rise to power. It's so obvious it's like a plot from a bad TV show, except this is all too real. Yep, definitely rethinking that promise not to beat him to death.

We are all dragging our butts to the practice arena the next afternoon. Coach gave us the morning off since most of the team stayed late at the hospital waiting for news about Robert. But the NHL is a business and doesn't stop for anyone. Tomorrow, we have a game, luckily home, so canceling practice altogether is out of the question. We have secured our playoff spot and currently sit first in our division, gaining home ice advantage. Not wanting to lose our position, we'll work hard to keep it.

When I enter the locker room, the team crowds around me for an update. Since anyone with eyes saw Catherine clinging to me in the hospital waiting room last night, the cat's pretty much out of the bag as far as our relationship goes, but I appreciate them keeping quiet about it anyway. There's still a somber feeling in the air, so no one makes any remarks about sleeping with the boss's daughter, thank God. I tell them the latest that there hasn't been any change. He'd had a good night, with no more episodes or ill effects from the surgery, and then we hit the ice.

We all skate a few laps, loosening our legs before Raki and I start stretching. Once we're good, we skate over to our goalie coach, Victor Sokolov, and his assistant coach, Dymtrus Tkachenko. When Russia invaded Ukraine, I wondered if there'd be bad blood between them, but it turns out Sokolov was livid and upset for Tkachenko, whose family still lives in Kyiv. There was a lot of Russian cursing about Putin that day. Even Raki joined in. If I was as talented at languages as Luka, I'm pretty sure I'd have learned some new colorful phrases.

I've never been so grateful for drills to take my mind off something in my whole life. Drills are a necessary evil. They give us goalies our speed, agility, and stability to make saves in all game situations. So, just like when I was in youth hockey, we practice T-pushes, butterflies, and slides. The only difference is the speed.

I skate aside as Raki takes the net. Coach and Tkachenko take turns shooting pucks his way. Nothing blindingly fast, just getting him moving so he blocks the pucks in all manner of ways.

"Cavie, you're up." Sokolov orders. Raki and I swap out.

My turn goes well, and Coach signals Raki to skate to the opposite goal on the other side of the ice. With the forwards done with their drills, it's time for them to give us a real test at speed. I tap my stick on the ice and then, with my glove, tap to both posts and the crossbar before turning and facing the line of players wanting to get the biscuit into my net. Some tendies talk to their nets, and some kiss the pipes. I prefer to let the pipes know I'm grateful they've got my back. All the D-men are standing off to the side, so it looks like we're starting with a breakaway setting.

Assistant Coach Eric Tawney blows his whistle. Bri and Foursie strike off at speed as they pass the puck back and forth. My eyes are on the puck, and Foursie makes his shot, trying for top shelf, but I deny him with a glove save that stings my hand.

"Damn, Fours, have you been upping your weight lifts?" I toss the puck to center ice because I hate it when the pucks start piling up. They distract me with superstitious bad luck.

"Don't you know it, Cavie."

They send more two on zeros at me until Tawney motions the D-men in. Cool, now I'll have help keeping the puck out of my net. The scrimmage heats, and so does the chirping.

"Keep your chin up, there's always beer league."

"Hey bud, I've seen better hands on a digital clock."

"Too bad that twig doesn't come with shooting lessons."

"Suck it, milk drinker."

"First time without toe picks, huh?"

Normally, we're not so vocal because the coaches want us

concentrating one hundred percent. I think they are letting it slide so we can all burn off the stress of worrying about our hospitalized owner. Mikey tries to crash my net and poke one through, but Holt is hot on his ass and strips the puck, icing it as the biscuit crashes the scrimmage on the other half of the rink.

"Great save, Holtie." I tap the ice with my stick in approval.

A slight smile curves his lips before he scowls and skates away. Ha. I broke through his wall. I've done it once. I can do it again. Now that I know his story, I'm going to let him know the Quakes have his back, whether he wants it or not.

Coach O'Ryan blows a long whistle, signaling the end of practice. The team's vibe has improved to something more normal. With smiles on most of our faces, we head off the ice. We're going to crush Anaheim tomorrow.

Jason Tolls intercepts me in the hallway, and I step aside, letting the team stragglers past.

"What's up, Tolli?"

"Hey," he lowers his voice. "I know this isn't the best time, but can we talk?"

"Sure, man." I may be hot and sweaty, but Tolls might be my new boss, so I'll take the time.

"Bishop spoke with me a few weeks back, and I'm excited." He grins. "Now that the offer is officially on the table to join player development, I was wondering if you made a decision yet."

I'd grab my neck if possible, but there's too much equipment in my hands. In truth, I haven't really thought about it. I meant to speak with Catherine, hear her thoughts, but I kept postponing. I'm still not sure I'm ready to give up my professional career, yet with our owner's heart attack, I think the writing's on the wall. Catherine is going to be the owner way sooner than later.

"Yeah, I have. I'll take it." In a flash, my life has changed.

"Awesome, man. You won't regret it."

"Thanks, Tolli. But can you keep this quiet? I'm not sure how this will affect the team, and we're on a record-breaking streak."

"No worries. There'll be no announcement until you're ready."

"Thanks, Jason." Keeping quiet also gives me an out, just in case. An escape hatch for a decision I'm torn about. Being a goalie is all I know and what I live for. I'm sure both Jason and Robert would understand if I changed my mind. I give him a nod and head for the locker room to shower and change. My heart races as I realize this might be my last season. I need to talk to Cat about it and get her take. No way can I tell the boys, they'd probably talk me out of it, and there's a small voice in my head telling me not to rush.

CHAPTER
Eighteen

CATHERINE

In the three long days since Dad's heart attack, I've memorized the view from his hospital room. I'm not complaining, the VIP room Dad's in is as nice as a hospital room can be. There's even good old faithful Alexa there to change the TV channel or play a song list. But all you see out the window is the parking garage and a hint of the tree-lined street below if you crank your head way, way, way, to the right. We're counting on Dr. Jones' estimate that he'll be ready to go home in the next couple of days. I'm sure he'll rest better in his own bed, without the endless string of noise that's inherent in a hospital, no matter if the door is closed or opened. Not to mention the antiseptic smell.

The huge bouquet the team sent adds not only a riot of color but also laces the air with the spicy scents of roses and stargazer lilies. I tuck my face into it one last time, thinking of Linc, before joining back in the ongoing debate that's raged on almost since Dad woke.

"You heard what the doctor said about your stress level,"

Mom reminds him again in that firm, steady voice that would be well-suited for a hostage negotiator.

"Yes, dear, so you've told me. Every day."

"And I will keep saying it until, like water over stone, I've worn you down." The corner of her lips migrates a fraction north from her frown as she bends down and kisses him.

"A man your age has no business putting in the hours you do, anyway," Daniel barks his opinion despite no one asking for it.

"Someone has to," I mutter under my breath. He turns to confront me, so maybe I wasn't as quiet as I thought. I don't care. He's been a giant pain in the ass from the moment Dad was hospitalized. Aloof and stand-offish in the waiting room, offering zero comfort to Mom, not to mention Joshie or me. He's been hovering in what he must think approximates a helpful way every day since. Only instead of helpful, he's bossy and overbearing, ordering around the staff like they are his personal flunkies. And I'm pretty sure when he takes a break to get something to eat, he's really getting a drink or three. There's only so much a breath mint can cover up.

Before we can dig our claws into each other, our little brother breezes through the door with a bright smile and a balloon bouquet featuring a floating hockey puck. In his other hand is an envelope. He takes in the scene of all of us engaged in our own conflicts and smiles even wider in a forced, joyless expression. "Ah, *la mia amorevole famiglia*, practicing for your *Game of Thrones* cosplay, I see."

As intended, the tension shatters, and we all chuckle. Except for Daniel, of course, who, from his furrowed brows, clearly has no idea what Josh is talking about. He was never the life of the party, but when did my big brother become an asshole *and* a complete dolt as far as pop culture goes? Mom and I both hug Josh, our little ray of sunshine, before giving him space to go to Dad's side.

We've been very blessed. This is the first time any of us

have had to deal with someone in our immediate circle being hospitalized with a serious illness. It could be because he's the youngest, but I suspect it's because he's the most innately sensitive to the needs of others, Josh has taken it the hardest. He covers it well. It's not like he's weeping or wailing, but he approaches Dad as if he's an illusion. A house of cards that will blow away to nothing if you touch him the wrong way and no one has told him what the right way is. He places the balloons on the table next to the flowers and approaches Dad like a child nervously walking to sit in Santa's lap. When he stops a foot short, Dad reaches out, takes his hand, and pulls him close.

"Come here, son, it's okay, your old man won't break," he murmurs into the top of his dark curly hair, and the fear that was keeping Josh stiff evaporates. His whole body relaxes as he hugs Dad back. Mom wraps her arm around me, and I realize Daniel is alone. Some of it is his choice. He could hug Mom from the other side, but I understand now he won't. I can't point to a specific incident that started the emotional distance, but his anger has been building over the years. That, plus his pride, will make getting through to him a huge mountain to climb.

"Did you get it?" Dad asks Josh.

"Yep." He opens the envelope and hands over a folded paper. "All ready for your approval."

Dad scans over the document and nods. "This will work." Josh smiles, and both their gazes lock to mine.

"What?" I glance over my shoulder, thinking there's something behind me, but nope, there isn't anything. When I look back, they are still staring at me.

"Here," my father offers me the paper. "I think you'll want to read this. It's a press release."

Okay. Obviously, the organization needs a statement about what's happening with the Quakes' owner. I assume it'll be a simple statement. He had a heart attack, but he's sure to make a full recovery. And it does say that until I get to the bottom, my eyes grow wide.

After careful consideration, Robert Bishop will be retiring at the end of this current season. He'll be transferring ownership of the Quakes to his daughter, Catherine Bishop. Ms. Bishop received her MBA at Wharton in Pennsylvania and has worked for the Quakes franchise for the past six years. The Quakes are proud to make history by having the first female owner of an NHL team leading the way in diversity.

Holy shit! It's finally happening. I'm stunned, eyes wide and jaw dropped. My father laughs.

"Congratulations, Catiebug. Your promotion is well deserved."

Josh takes a few steps from Dad's bedside and wraps me in a hug. "You're gonna kill it."

Mom smiles proudly, never leaving her chair by her husband. "I'm so proud of you, breaking down barriers not only for women but for people of color."

Daniel snorts. "Sure, she's a real trailblazer, the first female owner to fuck a player."

The room goes quiet, and the air crackles with tension. I inwardly flinch. He's not wrong. Nausea swamps me, putting a damper on my excitement.

"*Ingane,* there is no need for that kind of language," my mother commands.

"Is that how you see me? As a child?" Daniel's eyes turn cold and dark. "But apparently not the golden child anymore, right? Thanks, Dad, for your belief in me. You just made the worst mistake of your life. Don't come crawling to me when she lets you down."

Several emotions swirl in my gut as my brother stomps out the door. The joy that my lifelong dream is almost in my grasp, gratitude toward Dad and Mom for their confidence in me, and sorrow over the loss of a brother I still love despite it all. What hits the hardest is confusion, denial, and profound heartache over what to do about Linc.

✕

I invited Linc to come over for dinner tonight to break the news to him about Dad retiring before the PR department releases the information to the public. Nothing softens the blow of having to dump your boyfriend like a good meal, right? Not being the cook he is, nor a complete idiot, I ordered from a sushi restaurant he loves. He won't think I'm trying to take credit for their food since no one expects a normal person to make sushi, and I won't have the temptation to lie and say I made it.

My townhome isn't modest, like Linc's bungalow. It's actually kind of massive for a single person. The first floor is the three-car garage. The second floor has two bedrooms with their own en suites, also on that level is the laundry room. From the driveway, outside steps lead to the third, which is the main floor. It's an open concept like Linc's, but my living room is large, as is the kitchen. The floor-to-ceiling windows and sliding doors lead to my spacious backyard balcony. It features an ocean view, a fire pit, multiple outdoor seating areas, and a built-in BBQ with a sink. There are even countertops and storage below, which I confess I've never used. The fourth floor holds the main suite with its own excellent beach view, a much smaller balcony, and a fourth bedroom, which I converted into a home office. The view isn't as nice as the main bedroom, but you can still see the sparkling blue of the Pacific. My parents had talked me into the Manhattan Beach townhouse, even though I thought it was too big. They reminded me they'd hoped I would marry and have children. Fill my home with love. Besides, who could turn down the view?

This is the most nervous I've felt since…ever. Maybe that

time I had to come home and tell my parents that I had taken off the door of a police car with their new Range Rover was close, but this takes the cake. We understood that my becoming the owner would be an obstacle, but Linc and I both assumed we'd have a lot more time to figure this out. Now, with the end of the regular season only weeks away and the playoffs around the corner, it's all happening so fast. There's a squeezing in my chest like there's not enough oxygen in the room anymore.

Fly Me To The Moon resounds throughout the house. The former owner had installed the personalized doorbell tune, and the song amused me so much I never changed it. Besides, I have so few visitors I almost forget it's there.

I open the door to see the most gorgeous man I've ever known leaning against the doorframe. His dark gray Henley, matching his eyes, lies against his well-muscled chest. I've never been so envious of a piece of clothing in my life because wrapped around him, skin to skin, is exactly where I want to be. His worn jeans hug his strong legs. His gaze travels down my body, then back to my eyes. That single dimple of his is on full display as a lust-filled grin slides into place. Heat rushes to my face. My old, generic Quakes sweatshirt from a special fundraiser a few years ago hides every curve. I chose bright, multi-colored, capri-length leggings that clashed so I'd look as unsexy as possible. Too late. I remember he's color-blind and could smack myself. He wouldn't spot the clash because my clothing probably all looks gray. Even so, my hair is piled on top of my head in a messy knot, and I'm barely wearing any makeup. My purpose is to make him find me unappealing, making the split easier to swallow. How could this stunning man stare at me with that certain gleam in his eye? This is going to be harder than I thought.

"Hey, babe," he mumbles against my mouth as he plants his lips there, tongue darting in and out, playing with mine in a sizzling kiss. I want to push him off, but my arms don't have the strength to shove him away. Instead, my fingers curl into his soft hair as if they have a traitorous mind of their own.

He breaks the kiss and leans his forehead against mine. "Love you." Linc straightens and nudges me inside. With his foot, he shuts the door behind us. He makes a play at sniffing the air and grins. "Not smelling anything cooking, so it's takeout?"

I head toward the kitchen. "Ha, ha. Keep it up, big boy, and you won't get any Pisces sushi."

"Damn, woman. You drive a hard bargain. You know how much I love Pisces." He catches me, wrapping his arms around me from behind hugging me. "Have I told you lately how amazing you are?"

My muscles tense. How can I leave this man? Linc must have noticed the way my body stiffened. "Cat? Is everything all right with your dad?"

"He's good. Great, actually. He's being released tomorrow."

He gives me a full-body squeeze. "That's fantastic. And by the way, thanks for keeping me informed about his recovery. It helps the team calm down and focus more on our play. We'll miss him at the games, but with the ginormous TV at his house, he'll be even closer to the ice than in the owner's box."

I pull at his arms, which he loosens so I can step away and get some much-needed distance. I put the large granite island counter between us. "Yeah, that's not going to happen. Mom won't let him watch the games, not even the playoffs. Too much stress for his heart."

"Oh, ouch. What if we make it to the Cup final? That'll be easily a month away. It might be more torture and stressful not to watch."

"I guess time will tell. The Quakes have to make it

through round one first and then battle through two more to make it to the Cup."

Linc slaps a dramatic hand to his heart. "You wound me! Oh yee, of little faith."

I snicker as I pull out the sushi from the fridge and place the containers on the counter. Plates, chopsticks, and soy sauce are already out. He opens the wasabi and ginger boxes and then removes the lids from the sashimi and sushi. I pop open a beer for him, pour a glass of white wine for me, and then sit next to him on a bar stool.

He builds his wasabi and soy pool in the small *kobachi* bowl. I have no idea how he can use so much of the spicy green paste. Personally, I stay far away from it, although the memory of tasting it in his mouth when we've kissed in the past sends a streak of heat to the place I'm desperately trying to keep icy. I dip a piece of sashimi into my bowl of plain soy sauce and slip the salmon morsel into my mouth in an attempt to erase the memory from my mind. Right, like that's going to work. We eat in silence for a while, making a dent in our meal.

"So, Dad surprised me today." I might as well get this over with.

"He did? What's up?" He deftly picks up a piece of Toro, dunks it in his uber-spicy concoction, and pops the tender tuna into his mouth to chew.

I fill him in on everything, including Daniel's douchey response. I'm glad my brother isn't around, judging by the promise of violence in Linc's scowl. This next part will not improve his mood. My stomach sours, and I put down my chopsticks and stare down at my uneaten fish. There's no way I can meet his gaze. "I thought we'd have more time, but we'll have to end this, us being together, at the end of the season." The sigh that escapes me is a harsh exhale of depression. "Probably before then. Once the news is out, the scrutiny on me will be intense." I can't help the single tear from escaping. Damn, I was really hoping to keep it together.

"Hey," Linc swivels on his stool and pulls me onto his lap, wrapping me in his arms. I'm going to miss these arms and his displays of strength. I brush the stupid tear from my cheek. There is no excuse for being overemotional. We both knew this day would come.

"We need to talk about this. At least try to make this work. Your parents are excited about our relationship, and it's not like they didn't know you'd be the owner one day."

"But Daniel's not wrong. Dating a current player isn't the best optics."

He sighs. "I get that you want to be a positive role model, but does that mean you have to be some kind of vestal virgin?" He surprises a snort laugh out of me. "Why isn't it a great role model for young girls to see you display a healthy work-life balance? You know, the old bring home the bacon *and* fry it in the pan thing?"

"Maybe," I hedge, the first tendrils of hope curl around my heart.

"Come on, Cat. I love you, and I know you love me. Let's work it out. Give it a go." He makes me smile. "We're not living in the 50s or even the 80s. Women are allowed to be open about their sexuality. Fuck the double standards." His eyes go soft, and the tenderness in his gaze makes me wish for miracles. "Besides, I won't be a player forever, making the bacon thing way easier."

My resolve wavers. Nope, gotta do this for the team's sake, don't want to make them look bad.

"Look," he continues to press his case, "I was doing some research. There's Mario Lemieux, who owned *and* played for Pittsburgh, and no one thought that was a conflict of interest. Michael Jordan is part owner of the Washington Wizards and came out of retirement to play for them. There's an entire group of women players, some with their husbands and kids, who own a soccer team."

"In the National Women's Soccer League. That's a far cry from the NHL. And you clearly couldn't find one example of an owner sleeping with a player."

"Babe, up until you, all the NHL owners are old white dudes. For all we know, they're fucking players, silly. They just have great PR teams covering it up. For sure, they're doing the ice crews. My point is the times are changing. Slowly, but it is happening. Seriously, what message is it sending to girls if you are alone and isolated? That a woman can be successful in business, but only if they give up on love and having a family?"

"Welcome to being a woman in a man's world. Especially in professional sports. Sadly, that's what we have to do to succeed. And Linc, I do want to be successful."

"I know you do." He kisses my forehead. "And you will be. And I understand your concerns about how the public will view our relationship. What if I make this my last season?"

"What? No!"

"Jason Tolls offered me a spot in player development. I could take it. We could keep seeing each other."

I shake my head. "I won't let you give up your career for me. Your possible resentment later would kill us."

"But development is something I love doing, and every player's career has an expiration date. Lord knows I thought mine had expired earlier this season—"

"No, Linc, just no. You're killing it and will have other amazing seasons in you."

It's his turn to shake his head. "You're wrong, sweetheart. There's no way to predict I'll play at the level I am currently at next season. Shit happens. I'm fucking old for a hockey player and definitely past my sell-by-date. Each game is a gift. But what we have together? It doesn't have to end. No expiration required. I need you. I love you."

I can't hold his gaze, so I look down at my hands curled in my lap. He's willing to give up his career for me. Being a goalie is his life's blood. My heart starts beating too fast. My arguments crumble, and I know I'm losing a fight I never wanted to win in the first place. Because I do want it all. I want the team, but more importantly, I want Lincoln. He says he needs me, but really, it's me who needs him. I sigh and meet his tender gaze, grateful he gave me the time I needed to mentally work things out. Fearing the *what-ifs* is draining. I'm letting it all go. We'll work it out somehow. And if he's willing to retire for me, I certainly can take a little bad PR.

"Fuck the world and its narrow view. I choose us." His giant smile, including his dimple, makes me laugh, the joy bubbling out of me. His wanting to fight for us deserves a reward, and I know just the thing. I slide off his lap, grab his hand, and tug. Linc comes off his stool and follows me to my large, comfortable sectional couch.

I give him a playful push, and he goes with it, landing on the edge of the sofa. Perfect. I nudge between his knees, which he parts, and I step closer. Giving him what I hope is a wicked smile, I sink to my knees.

"Cat." His voice is rough and low as I reach for his belt. In seconds, I have the pliant leather stripped and tossed to the floor. I peek through my lashes and see his gaze fixated on my hands. Next, I pop the button on his jeans and carefully slide the zipper down, stroking my hand over his erection bulging behind his black boxer briefs. A hiss escapes him, and I grin. "Tease."

"You love it," I answer his growled word. Grabbing his waistband, as well as his boxers, I tug down. "A little help, please. And lose your shirt."

Linc chokes on a laugh. "Yes, ma'am." He crunches his

stomach muscles as he lifts his hips while pulling off his shirt. Oh yum, his eight-pack is on display.

I get his clothes to his ankles and tug them off his feet, pushing them aside. Gazing at him, I take in all two hundred pounds of muscled, ripped perfection with his hard shaft waiting for my attention. It's like his cock knows I'm appreciative because it twitches. I need my hands on that bad boy. Wrapping my fingers around the base, I give a tight squeeze before stroking him. A growl of approval escapes Linc's throat. My own blood heats. I love how I'm affecting him, and I am. A pearl drop of pre-cum glistens from his tip, making me lick my lips.

Lowering my mouth, my tongue flicks out, lapping up his arousal. His salty flavor spikes my taste buds, making my pulse throb and my panties wet. I wrap my lips around his tip and suck hard. He rewards me with a moan.

"Cat," he groans my name as he threads his fingers into my hair. "More. Swallow me down."

I shiver at his rough command, and my thighs clench, seeking relief. Later. Right now, it's all about him. One hand grips him tight while I take him to the back of my throat, pressing my tongue along his sensitive vein. With my free hand, I play with his balls. They are high and tight, a sign he's close. It never takes much to get him to climax with my mouth. He claims he's never had better. I think it's more about the emotional connection because I know my skills are lacking, but I make up for it with enthusiasm.

Bobbing up and down, I suck when he's deepest. I feel like torturing him a bit, so I remove my lips with a pop, and he groans. Linc knows my game of drawing out his release. I lick him over the tip and then down, following his popped vein. He's silky satin over hard steel. The musk of his arousal fills my nose, and I moan. His hold on my hair tightens, sending a jolt of pleasure straight to my pussy.

I swallow him down, moaning. I need his climax. It calls

to me. Making sure I stroke on the part I can't take, I work him over.

"Catherine."

Humming in the back of my throat, I work him harder and am rewarded. He comes gloriously, and I swallow his release down. When he collapses onto the couch, I let him drop from my mouth and lick my lips. His eyes are closed, and he's breathing hard. All indications I've done an excellent job. I smile. The perfectionist in me is happy with my results.

He opens his heavy-lidded eyes, staring at me. "I love you."

"Love you, too."

"You have too many clothes on."

He stands and grabs my ass, lifting me. I wrap my legs around his waist while laughing. Linc loves carrying me and probably hopes I'd prefer never to walk anywhere on my own. My hands grasp his shoulders, and I go in for a kiss. His mouth devours mine as our tongues duel. Our kiss breaks as he heads for the stairs and the bedroom.

"What about the sushi?"

"Forget the fish. I want my turn," he growls.

Smiling, I look forward to his efforts. He won't disappoint, as he's proving over and over again. I really hope our future is bright and we will work out.

X

The office is abuzz when I get in, and it's not even seven-thirty. The press release went out at four this morning to make the East Coast news, and the phones are all ringing off the hook. Especially since most of the staff aren't in the office yet.

Around the corner, a jittery Geoffrey Carter paces outside my door. *Crap.* I was hoping for one last peaceful morning before having to deal with this shit. I have enough on my

plate with the news of me becoming the Quakes' owner without having to deal with Carter's attitude. I halt in front of him and raise an eyebrow.

"Can we talk?"

"Sure, why not?" I gesture to my office and open the door, flicking on the lights. He follows me in. Taking a seat behind my desk, I motion him to sit across from me, which he does.

"Are you firing me?"

Well, he certainly got straight to the point. I sigh. I thought about this for days now and dreamed of it, if I'm being honest, for the past year. How sweet my day would be without Carter. However, my dad is far from stupid and wouldn't have kept Carter on all these years if he was a terrible GM. I respect my father enough to give the man a chance, though there will be conditions.

"No, I won't be letting you go." He nods, thinking he's off the hook. "However, there is at least one condition for me keeping you on."

"And that's…"

"If I hear from any of our female employees, just one complaint, I will fire your ass. Your misogynistic ways end today. I won't tolerate it." I stare him down. "If you treat me or any other woman like we're idiots and beneath you, you're gone. Is that clear?"

He stares at me while I match his gaze. Carter probably has no idea what a misogynist is. I'll give him time to look it up. "Yes, I understand."

"Great." I stand, and he does so as well. "If that's all, I've got work to do."

"Yeah, we're done." He heads for the door but pauses and glances back. "Congratulations, Catherine." With those gritted words, he exits.

I collapse into my chair. Glad that's over with. He'll be on a tight leash, and I'll certainly check in with my female employees to make sure he is in compliance. Mostly, we only disagreed about my not having a penis being a hindrance, so maybe we can work together if he cleans up his act. For the stability of the team, I'll keep him for next season. After that? Who knows?

With that horrible task over, I sit at my desk and hunker down to handle the top priorities Dad was dealing with before his heart attack. I log into my computer, pull up the proposal for next season's television rights, and start reading.

"May I come in?" I jump at the sound of Daniel's voice, not expecting anyone in for another half an hour at least. While I've already been woken with incredible sex, hit the gym, and am dressed in a suit, he's in the same sports coat and tie that I swear I saw him in yesterday. Only much more rumpled, like he slept in them. There's at least one day's worth of beard stubble on his jaw, and his eyes are so red it looks like he's recently been maced. And, of course, the odor of cheap alcohol permeates the room.

"My God, Daniel, you need to get help." I meant to deliver my admonishment in a stern voice but can barely manage a whisper. He looks like hell. "What happened to you?"

He burbles a mirthless sound that might have started as a laugh. "You mean last night or in general? Because last night I hid out in a dive bar, and then the alley behind it, until dawn. In general, your fucking team started winning despite all the experts betting the lack of a goalie would sink them. Already a little behind to some nasty people, I put everything I had on the Quakes losing. Then your fucking Cavanaugh starting playing like a Hall of Famer, and now I'm a dead man."

"You bet against the Quakes?" The outrage in my voice isn't just about personal loyalty. It could be illegal. Well, probably not. It would be if he actually worked for the Quakes' organization. It's definitely illegal for a player to bet. At any rate, if it got out that Daniel Bishop was betting on hockey, it *would* reflect badly on our team.

"I just told you the sharks are circling to get their pound of flesh, and of course, your concern is with your precious Quakes. So typical of you, the Perfect Princess."

His words hurt less than his ugly tone, dripping with disgust. How did I miss the depth of Daniel's hatred for me? Or maybe I didn't. This isn't my brother talking or his actions. He's sick, obviously, an alcohol and gambling addict.

"I've lost it all. Wife, money, Dad called me for a meeting later in the week, no doubt to fire me, fuck you very much."

"Me? How is this my fault? You did this to yourself."

"Whatever. Point is I have nothing left, while you get everything you've ever wanted. Your fucking hockey team, your goalie. Well, if I have to lose, you do too."

A cold chill races down my spine. He hasn't been showing it lately, but Daniel is a smart, cunning, ruthless businessman when he's on top of his game. His voice holds a piece of the steely edge that helped him expand Bishop Tech, but there's a jagged, off-the-rails quality to it. Eyes narrowing at him, I ask warily, "What are you talking about?"

He gives me an ugly sneer, places his phone on my desk, and plays a voice memo he's probably had cued since he drank enough courage to confront me.

"*My name is Rainbow Raine. I'm the ex-wife of that sick mother-fucker, Lincoln Cavanaugh, and I do solemnly swear that while we were together, he was physically and emotionally abusive.*" The way her high-pitched voice stumbled over the words, making it clear she was reading off of a script, but still, I felt the blood drain from my face. "*If they lost a game, he'd take it out on me, always careful to hit where the bruises wouldn't be seen. If they won, it was even worse. He would do things to me sexually that were...um.*"

Daniel shut the recording off before she could finish. My guess is she faltered because she was thinking about how great the sex was and forgot her lines. "It goes on for another fifteen minutes or so, where she details all the sexually deviant stuff he made her do, including a three-way with another man."

A laugh burst out of me before I could stop it. "You're kidding, right? No one is going to believe that crap."

He shrugs as if he didn't have a care in the world, an ugly sneer still fixed in place. "Are you willing to gamble your boy toy's future on it? I give this to every idiot with a hockey podcast or blog, and within a day, millions of people will hear this. Even if only half believe him, he'll be the most hated man in hockey."

"Don't be absurd. How did you get her to record that, anyway?"

"It's surprising how little cash it takes for a jilted wife to get the fifteen minutes of fame she thinks she's owed. Tramp thinks this is going to make her a star somehow."

Another lie upon lie. Rainbow left Linc for an AHL player. It was public knowledge at the time. My shoulders sag. I'm sure this problem is easily solved with a payout, but the bigger issue is how to get Daniel the help he needs. This is going to break our parents' hearts as if they weren't dealing with enough right now. "How much do you want?"

"Oh no, little sister, I don't want your money."

My skin pebbles from a sudden chill. If this isn't about money, what does he really want? A bad feeling sinks into the pit of my stomach, making me nauseated. "Then what, the team? You want me to give you the team?"

"Too late for that. I know I can't have the Quakes. Dad would never let you walk away. There isn't a good enough excuse." He slams his fist on my desk. "I've lost everything, so now you have to lose something. You cut loose the goalie or watch him be destroyed."

"What?" My tongue is thick and numb in my mouth. "What are you talking about?"

"Oh please, you think you're so clever with your tricks, sneaking around. The looks you give each other are so obvious." He falters, sorrow washing over him. "The way Shannon used to look at me."

I grasp at the straw that he still loves his wife. "Yes, I admit it, Linc and I are in love."

A triumphant grimace slithers across his face. "That's why you have to dump him."

"I don't understand. Why are you doing this? We were close once. Why are you taking away my shot at happiness?" Staring at him, he looks ill. He is ill. When did he become an alcoholic? And gambling? He needs help.

"Because I can." He stands and points a finger at me. "Ditch the goalie, or I'll ruin him."

He storms out of my office, slamming the door behind him. I can't believe what just happened. What the hell? My whole body shakes, and I'm chilled to the bone. What am I going to do? I don't doubt for a second he'll follow through. I have to protect Linc. The need to keep him safe floods me. Even if he retires, this story would ruin his chances of getting any sort of coaching or announcing gig. He probably couldn't get a job bagging groceries with the label "wife beater" following him wherever he went.

I want to run to my father, but I can't. He's only getting out of the hospital today and already has a damaged heart. Despair crushes me. I have to break it off. Too bad Daniel doesn't want the team because I realize now I'd walk away from my dream in order to protect Lincoln. He doesn't deserve what my brother has planned.

Fisting my hands to quell the shaking, a sudden thought strikes me. How in the world do I make the break up believable? Especially since only last night, I let him talk me into giving our relationship a real try. Fuck me. I better come up with something because I already know Linc will fight for us.

CHAPTER
Nineteen

LINCOLN

I hand my keys to the valet with a warning about taking care of my classic car. Then, with one last tug at my shirt collar that's strangling me, I enter Oto on 8th. I'm confused why Cat asked me to meet her here since this upscale restaurant is far from the low profile we've been trying to keep. Money drips off the other patrons, with men in their Brunello Cucinelli suits and the women decked out with Harry Winston diamonds. I figure, at least, there probably aren't a lot of hockey fans here.

The *maitre de* shows me to our table, and I'm stunned, as always, at how beautiful Catherine is. Even in a simple black dress and very little jewelry, she outshines every woman in the room. I take her hand and press my lips to her knuckles. She grimaces, her gaze darting around as if worried about people seeing us. Okay, that's weird since she's the one who asked me to join her here for dinner. A trill of confusion ripples through me, so I shake it off with a light-hearted approach.

"Hey babe, what's the occasion? Are we celebrating your dad getting out of the hospital?"

"No," she huffs out. "He's far too frail still to be celebrating anything. In fact, seeing him like that yesterday taught me a very important lesson."

Suddenly, my mouth feels dry for some reason, so I take a sip of water. Out of the corner of my eye, I see the waiter approaching and wave him off with a curt shake of my head. The way he pivots and disappears says he has the same feeling I do—something isn't right. "What lesson is that?" I touch her hand, and she slides her fingers out of my reach.

"That life is far too short to waste one single minute of it on frivolous pursuits."

Now I'm seriously confused because I have no fucking idea where this conversation is going. "What frivolous pursuit are we talking about here?"

She shoots me an unfiltered eye roll I've only ever seen her give Daniel. The one that says, *Duh, how dumb can you be, asshole?* I don't know how she packs so much harshness in such beautiful eyes, but the message is clear. "Us. This so-called relationship is guaranteed to lead nowhere good."

Confusion gives way to anger. "Are we back to this old argument? You having to choose between me or the team? I thought we settled that the other night."

She shakes her head and gives me an icy smile. "No, it's not about that. You were right, fuck 'em if they want to stick to those double standards. They have no right to judge me. I'm a Bishop."

"Then I don't understand what's wrong. You love me, and I love you, so why this charade?" I'm getting frustrated beyond belief with this conversation, this act she's putting on.

"Didn't you just hear me? I'm a Bishop. This"—she waves her hand to indicate the ostentatious surroundings—"is my world, not some beer joint with corn hole games. I'd let myself get swept up in our...romance, I guess you can call it, but Dad's heart attack reminded me we could all go at any minute. And at the end of the day, the person with the most toys wins, and I deserve a winner. I mean, you're hot and a really great fuck." She puts enough emphasis on the word to earn glares and curious glances from the tables on either side, but neither of us cares enough at this point to take the volume down a notch. "But my five-year plan doesn't include nursing a broken-down jock who can't even dress properly because he's too blind to recognize blue from green."

My blood boils, and I get a firsthand lesson about what it means to be hot under the collar. I yank off the tie and unbutton the top button of my shirt. Fuck this, let them try to throw me out for not wearing the damn tie. "Why are you saying all of this? I know this isn't you. You told me so on our first date in the park when we ate from the food truck."

The scorn in her eyes is so acidic I wince. "Please, I was lying through my teeth. My parents raised me to be better than to mock those less fortunate than us."

But there's a crack in her facade. I'm almost certain of it. A glimmer of something in her eyes when I brought up that night on the grass at Echo Park Lake, where we had our first kiss. "Nope, I'm not buying it. You could have called me or come over to my place to tell me all of this in person. This isn't you, trying to humiliate me in public."

"Because I have to be blunt to get through your thick head that I've changed my mind. Otherwise, you'd keep trying to talk me into giving us a shot. Yes, you were very convincing, especially that part with your tongue on my clit." This time, audible gasps resound from the table next to us, although the wife looks more envious than shocked. "But doesn't the fact that I needed to be convinced tell you anything about us? I realize now that the moment I'm not feeling that magnificent cock of yours, I've lost interest."

She takes a sip of her wine and places the glass down with delicate care. "I can't blame Daniel for his addictions, I guess, since I have one of my own. I get off on having inappropriate relationships. The first time was back in grad school when I slept with my college professor, but there were others. Lots of others. That's why I'm so attracted to you. It's the danger and salaciousness of it all. But. I'm not getting any younger, and with my dad's heart attack? It made me realize it's time to end the fun and games. I need to find a man who can give me a future, if fewer thrills."

I stare at her, stunned. This isn't Catherine. But maybe I didn't know her at all? I haven't had the best track record with women, and this conversation is giving me flashbacks of when Rainbow handed me divorce papers. A shock from out of the blue.

"That's the other reason I asked you to meet me here. Frankly, we've been here before. You'd look at me with those sad eyes, start touching me, and I'd love it, I really would, and then change my mind again. But the truth is, I need a man who is at least as smart as I am. You were right, you know, when you accused me of being in this for the sex. I just didn't realize it until now."

My hands clenched in rage. It's all I can do not to flip the table over. But it's my fault for being so stupid. How did I not see through the act? Because she's right, the fact that I had to keep talking her into fighting for us should have told me there's no *us* to fight for. She said all I needed to hear when she refused to have lunch with me, but I wanted this woman so much I ignored what my brain told me and made decisions with my heart. Or, more accurately, my dick. Neither of them gets to be in charge of anything from here on out.

This is so Rainbow all over again. I'm only good enough to be a fling, nothing more. And oh yeah, the team of Dick and Heart were the ones driving that bus, too. Thank God I never told her about my deal with her father and Tolli to retire at the end of the season and move into Quakes' player development. That's not happening. No way do I want to be in the same building as this viper.

"You know what?" I lean over the table and keep my voice low. If she wants to shock people, that's her game, not mine. "You're right. You deserve someone as much of an asshole as you are. Because no pussy, not even one as fine as yours, is worth this back-and-forth bullshit. Why don't you call that douche I saved you from that night and see if he's free? He seems like a real charmer." And to prove her wrong that I'm not a thug in a suit, I stand and walk out with dignity I'm pulling from somewhere deep inside. Although from the way the staff and other patrons hustle to give me a wide berth, there's a much darker emotion written all over my face.

X

We're in the last eight minutes of the third period as I watch our boys battle in the O-zone against the Florida Sun Flares. It's been six days, and I'm still so pissed at Catherine for using me like that. But the good thing is, at least we're on an extended road trip, so I don't have to see her. I straighten in the crease when I notice a breakaway heading my way. And, of course, one of the two Sun Flares is fucking number Nineteen. He's been up my ass all night. If he tries one more slash or cross check on me, he's going down.

I block the shot, and it bounces to the boards. By now, our D-men have caught up, and there's a battle to gain puck control. *Bam*! My head snaps to the right, and my helmet goes flying as number Nineteen skates past me. The fucker hit me in the head. Whether by fist or elbow, I'm done. Throwing down my stick, I grab the back of Mitchelson's jersey, spin him around, and start throwing punches. He's game, and the fight's on. I take a hit on my chin before managing to drop my blocker and glove, and then the players from both sides pile on, and we have a melee.

I trip Mitchelson and take him down to the ice for one last punch to his face before the Ref pulls me off. Funtime is over. The fight had me feeling awesome, which has been missing since Catherine stomped all over me. The head referee pushes me toward the bench.

"You're done, Cavanaugh. Game misconduct for throwing punches with your blocker. Get your ass off the ice."

"What about Mitchelson? He fucking punched me in the head, and he's been slashing and cross checking me all night."

"Not your concern. Get off my ice."

Connor has the gate open for me and pats my shoulder as I pass the bench. "Way to take the asshole down, Cavie. But next time, drop your blocker first."

I don't acknowledge him. When I get to the tunnel, I see Alexandr kitted up and stretching. I pause. "Take care of my crease. No pucks in."

"*Da*. I'll keep it safe."

We fist bump, and I head to the locker room. I'm not too worried. There's only like five minutes left in the game, Raki's got it covered. I strip down and shower. In ten minutes, I'm dressed in my suit, seated on the bench, and watching the rest of the game on the monitor in the room. My anger has evaporated, and all I feel is a weird, sad numbness. Coach is going to read me the riot act, and right now, I have zero fucks to give.

As the clock winds down and the end game horn sounds, a small smile quirks my lips. True to his word, Raki didn't let any pucks in, and we win, four to two. Soon, the sounds of the team reach the visitor's locker room before the door bangs open, and they jubilantly stride in. Someone hits the playlist, and celebratory music pounds through the paired sound system.

Coach enters and points at me. With a sigh, I stand and follow him down the hall to an office. I grab a chair and sit as he paces.

"You had valid reasons for going after Mitchelson, that was a righteous takedown. I only wished you dropped your blocker first." He stops his pacing and braces his hip on the desk. "You're playing even more like a madman, making those incredible saves, so I can't scream at you for your game."

"Good to know, Coach."

"However,"—he runs his hand down his face—"I've known you for far too long not to recognize when something's wrong. Talk to me."

"Nothing's wrong, nothing's going on, Coach. And just now, you stated that my game's improved."

He blows out a frustrated sigh. "I can't help you if you don't tell me, Linc." I shrug. "Fine, my door is always open. Get your ass out of here and celebrate with the team."

With a nod, I stand and enter the locker room to cheers, fist bumps, and slaps on the back. The goodwill and support of my team almost makes my anger and heartache disappear. Almost.

X

Back at the hotel, I slink off to my room instead of hitting a local club or bar. It was hard ditching the players' various invitations, but I have my ways. I strip out of my suit and replace it with cotton sweatshorts and a T-shirt. Earlier, I placed a room service order through their hotel's website for a bottle of scotch, and I hope it gets here soon.

I pace, filled with restless energy, when a knock on my door halts me in my stride. Finally. I wrench the door open without looking through the peephole. My mistake. Standing in the hallway are Zach, Luka, and Brian. Oh, fuck me.

Brian holds a bottle of Scotch in his hand. "We intercepted your delivery."

With those words, the three men push past me and enter my room without so much as a by-your-leave. I let the door slam before turning and facing the music. This should be fun.

Bri breaks the seal on the bottle. "Edradour, nice choice." He starts pouring rounds for everyone.

"Guys, I appreciate whatever this is but—"

"Sit," Zach commands, shoving me to the bed. I've got three inches and a dozen pounds on him, plus bulk, but when he turns on that "captain, my captain" voice, it's hard to ignore him. The fierce look in his eyes says he's not messing around, so I stay seated. It doesn't mean I have to meet his gaze. I do the rebellious teen thing and roll my eyes at him. It doesn't get me any further than it used to get me with my old man. "What the hell is wrong with you?"

"Nothing," I mutter back, but the overused reply sounds tired even to me.

Ribi calls me something in one of the five languages he speaks, and I don't have to understand the word to catch from the tone he called me an asshole. "You got thrown out of the game for misconduct. I know," he raises his hand to stop my argument, "Mitchelson is a fucker and deserved it, but you'd never risk a game for a petty vendetta." He accepts his Scotch and grins. "Putting the smack down is Holtie's job."

Brian sits on the bed next to me, hands me my Scotch but doesn't clink glasses in the traditional toast. "Dude, you're losing it. You've been an angry dickhead who's impossible to live with ever since you and Catherine split, and it's getting worse, not better."

What can I say? He's right. So I put my mouth to better use than a pointless argument and down the drink instead. It leaves a wonderful, smokey burn in my throat but doesn't numb the pain.

Zach pulls the chair from the desk in the room, turns it so the back is toward me, and straddles it. "Cavie, how long have we been friends?"

"Thirteen years," I mumble, still unable to look him in the eye. Because they're right, I risked the team losing a game, and right now, every win counts. We're just lucky we have a tendie of Raki's ability, especially this late in the season. Most teams aren't as fortunate. "I was stupid to risk the game. It won't happen again."

"We don't give two shits about the game," Zach barks at me, so much anger vibrating through his words that his Swedish accent becomes pronounced. "We're worried about you."

"You have been behaving like a bear with a burr in its butt," Ribi adds in what I can only guess is some Slovenian folksy saying.

When Brian chips in his two cents, he sounds sad, almost wistful, rather than angry. "You were the happiest I've ever seen you when you were with Catherine. And she felt the same way, I'm certain of it. We talked at the fundraiser, and honestly, I hope a woman looks at me someday the way she looked at you. So whatever you did, fix it."

"That's just it," I shout, exploding off the bed to refill my glass. "I didn't do anything. The high and mighty Ms. Bishop informed me over dinner at Oto on 8th that I wasn't good enough for her long-term game plan. That I was a nice fuck, but not boyfriend material."

"How was the food?" Ribi asks, "I've always wanted to try it." The guys look at him, and he shrugs. "What? I'm just asking?"

"Don't know, we never even ordered." I slam the bottle down.

Zach shifts his focus back to me. "That doesn't make

sense. She was easing your relationship out into the open. Even Jenny commented that you weren't her dirty little secret anymore. Something had to have happened."

"It could be her father's heart attack shook her more than she's letting on," Bri offered. "The two of them are pretty tight."

I'm ashamed to say that hadn't occurred to me in the six days I've been letting this hurt fester inside me. Could it be related somehow? Then I remember the ugly look on her face when she said, unless my cock is inside her, she has no interest in someone like me. *A dumb jock* was the unspoken part. "No, man, she came out and said nursing a broken-down goalie wasn't in her five-year plan, whatever the fuck that is."

The guys suck in a collective hiss. "*Sranje,*" Ribi mutters.

"I don't know, dude," Brian slowly adds. "I'm not buying it. This is a complete one-eighty. Have you considered talking with her, give her a call?"

"No. A huge fucking giant, no." I gulp my Scotch and leap to my feet to pour another, except Zach snatches the bottle before I can get to it. I spin and glare at my friends. "She's all lies, just like Rainbow. Apparently, illicit affairs are her particular kink." I throw my hands into the air. "The one thing she said was correct. It was *always* me having to fight for us, *me* talking her around. I'm done."

Zach shakes his head. "Catherine is not Rainbow. Nothing like her at all. Stop being an angry, sullen, stubborn asshole. Find out what's at the bottom of all this. We want you to be happy."

"I'm done talking. In fact, I can't be around her. I'm going to ask for a trade."

The collective "What!" echoes off the walls as they run their mouths off as one.

"No way, you can't."

"Don't let your emotions make choices."

"Nehaj biti neumen kurac."

I need a drink, so I try to snatch the Scotch bottle, but Zach tosses it to Luka, who grins. "Let me translate, asshole—stop being a dumb fuck. You can have another drink when you get your head screwed back on."

"Fuck you all." I give them my back and walk to the window, staring out at Sunrise, Florida's cityscape. Now I wish I'd gone out to a club and gotten laid instead of this shitty intervention. There's no way I'm telling the boys about the position Robert, Tolli, and I talked about in player development. They'd use it as ammunition to get me to stay, plus say it's a way to keep Catherine. It wasn't about the owner/player optics. She's done with me. The boys weren't at that restaurant. They didn't see her, hear her. My stomach rolls. I'm going to ask for a trade and get the hell out of Los Angeles.

✕

I collapse on my hotel bed in Philadelphia, fucking exhausted. Thursday night, after getting thrown out of the Florida game, my boys wouldn't leave me alone. They called me a stubborn asshole, dropped the conversations about both the trade and Catherine, and then let me get hammered. Brian stayed with me last night to make sure I caught the team bus to the airport for our next game. Thank God it's a travel day with no skate practice, at least not until the next morning when there's light skate. After tomorrow's game, we have one more on the road before going home for our final two games in the regular season.

My head is still pounding, even though the amounts of electrolytes and water I've drunk should have fixed my hangover. I pull out my phone and stare at the locked screen. It's a selfie of Catherine and me taken on our first date, sitting on the lawn holding our fish tacos. I need to change this. The photo kills me each and every time. I've got to end this. Fuck it. I'm doing it now. We don't meet for dinner for another four hours, and our GM should be available in Los Angeles. I unlock the screen, find Carter in my contacts, and dial. I need out of the Quakes, and he's the man who can make this happen.

He answers on the third ring. "Geoffrey Carter."

"Hey, it's Lincoln Cavanaugh."

There's a pause. "Is there a problem?"

"Yeah, sort of." I pinch the bridge of my nose, willing the pounding in my head to go away.

"Lincoln, I'm going to need more. What can I do for you?" I hear the impatience in his voice but don't give two fucks.

"I want a trade. As soon as possible." If a new team picks me up, I can ask about going into that team's player development when I retire. It'd be awesome if the Frosts took me. I could be close to my family. What I'm not prepared for is his laughter. "Stop laughing, Carter. I'm serious."

He collects himself. "I'm not laughing at you, just the circumstances. I wanted to trade your ass so badly, but then you started killing it, and that went out the window."

"But that should be good, right? There has to be someone who needs a hot netminder."

"I fielded calls before the deadline from teams wanting you, but we can't lose you now while we're in the playoff run. With you in tandem with Alexandr, we've won our division mathematically, even if we lose a few of these last games. Besides, if you're traded now, you couldn't play for your new team until next season."

I grab the back of my neck and try to keep the frustration out of my voice. "What about after the season? You can find me a team then, right?"

"No, I can't." Carter heaves out a sigh. "I'm sorry, Lincoln. It's not possible. Robert was dead set against trading you earlier when you sucked. He's certainly not going to go for it now. I highly doubt Catherine will, either."

Yeah, I wouldn't bank on that. I'm sure she'd love for me to go somewhere else. Or maybe not. With her cold ass bitchiness, she'd want what's best for the team, which means keeping my ass. Retiring seems to be the only path left to me. "There's nothing you can do?"

"Sorry, no."

Fuck me. I guess I'm retiring. I'll move back to Minnesota and figure out what the hell to do with the rest of my life. Not that I have to work. I've earned a lot of money with my NHL career and invested wisely. But I'd go crazy sitting on my ass all day.

"If you're serious, call Robert. Technically, he's still the owner until after the playoffs. Convince him, and I'll be able to make a trade I'm sure will be beneficial for the Quakes."

"Thanks, Geoff, I appreciate the advice. Sorry to waste your time."

We disconnect, and I'm staring at my phone again. If I'm doing this, there's no time like the present. I dial Robert Bishop's number. He answers after the first ring.

"Lincoln, is everything okay?"

"Not really, sir."

"Robert." He chuckles.

"Robert. I'm sorry to disturb you. How are you doing?"

He laughs. "I'm climbing the walls. Everyone is treating me as if I'm glass, and it's driving me crazy. I feel great."

"That's awesome." My heart pounds in time with my head. How do I tell him I want out? He's been nothing but supportive. Does he even know about Catherine breaking up with me?

"Linc, what's wrong? Talk to me."

And so I do.

CHAPTER
Twenty

CATHERINE

"Suck it, Jason Segel, you don't know anything about heartbreak," I sob between mouthfuls of Americone Dream, lobbing a wadded tissue at the television. "You could have Rachel, you big dumbass, but all you want is the one person you can't have." Yeah, because I'm totally talking about the movie now. It's Friday night, and Brittany kidnapped me from work. She said she was tired of the sad recluse act I've been keeping this week at my house, and we needed a change of scenery. So here we are, at Brittany's place, a compromise so I can cry my makeup off and let my hair down without scandal or pitying looks from the public. And as my bestie said, she's sick of my townhouse.

"Okay, my bad," Brittany admits as she pulls the carton of ice cream out of my hand. Who needs bowls when you go to your bestie's for a shoulder to cry on? Gone are the two business people in suits and heels. We're dressed like the college roommates we once were in stretchy pants and T-shirts, no make-up, and hair in messy ponytails. There's a pile of used tissues scattered at my feet. She scoops out a serving of ice cream the size of a dime. Wimp. "I heard *Forgetting Sarah Marshall* was funny. I should have checked the plot first."

She shuts off the movie, grabs her wine glass, and focuses on me. "It's been a week, Cat, and you've eaten your way through the top five Ben & Jerry's selections. This is nuts. You need to talk to Linc and tell him about Daniel's threat."

"Great idea. Then I can visit the man I love in prison, doing life for killing my worthless brother." I punctuate the thought with another heaping spoonful, digging deeper to get a chunk of waffle cone.

She gets off the couch and pads barefoot to the kitchen to pour herself some more wine. The first night Brittany came over taught us that if we brought the bottle into the living room, it would be gone before we knew it. I switched to eating thoughtlessly rather than drinking, considering the state I last saw my brother in.

"So what's your big plan, then? Eat so much ice cream you slip into a coma, wake up, and fall for Linc's brother like in that something sleeping movie with Sandra Bullock?"

There's no point in correcting her that she got the plot of *While You Were Sleeping* all wrong, so I don't, stuffing my face with more ice cream instead. Just thinking about how happy Sandy's character was at the end of that movie when she gets the man she loves starts me sobbing all over again.

"Okay, that's it," Brittany announces, yanking the carton out of my hand, putting the top back on, and shoving it back in the freezer of her ultra-sleek, modern, and completely unused kitchen. "If you don't stop this pity party, we're going to have to do retail therapy not for fun but because you've gained fifteen pounds, and that's not going to solve anything. What does Josh have to say about all of this?"

"He's at a marketing conference in Atlanta that was scheduled ages ago. Mom and Dad both insisted he go, and I didn't want to add to his turmoil. Especially after seeing his Instagram post relaxing with friends at the convention. Besides, there's nothing to solve, B." I blow my nose, which is running again. I've gone through two boxes of Kleenex this week. My nose is so red my assistant asked if I wanted her to get me cold medicine. If only I could take a pill for what's wrong with me. "I have to stay away from Linc to protect him. And even if I was willing to risk Daniel releasing that clearly staged tell-all from his bitchy ex-wife, Linc will never talk to me again."

"You don't believe that," she wraps her arm around me. "He loves you. Just explain, well, not everything because you're right, he'd definitely kill Daniel, but at least about the Rainbow threat. You need to come clean and tell him why you did what you did, plus be ready to take that cow to court."

I shake my head, the replay of the hatred and disgust on Linc's face that night at the restaurant comes back to me in Technicolor. "You didn't see him. I had to hurt him to make the story stick, and you know what an overachiever I am."

"So you said. Nice touch with the fictional affair with a college professor, by the way. But you're miserable, and from the way he nearly killed that guy on the Florida team, he's not in his happy place, either. You're the only one who can fix this."

She's right about all of it. But I know Linc. Even if it was possible to be with him and both of us survive the Rainbow shit storm, it would take a miracle for him to forgive me. And that will never happen. I'd need a grand gesture of epic proportions, but since my life isn't a romantic comedy, I'm shit out of luck.

X

Curled on the couch, continuing my pity-fest with a warm bowl of mac-n-cheese, I'm waiting for the second period to start. I'm dressed in my stretchy yoga pants, thick fuzzy socks, and the softest Quakes' hoodie I own because even with the heater on, I'm cold. I'd have Brittany over to watch the game, but hockey is so not her thing, and I've pushed our friendship boundaries enough this week. Plus, it's Saturday evening, and she's out trolling for men, something I have absolutely no desire to be a wingperson for.

We're tied with the Liberties at one-one. The Philly players have been rough on our team, and I can see the frustration building. Holt has spent more time in the sin bin than on the actual ice. A fight is bound to happen. The puck drops, and Zach wins the face off. I'm so glad Linc is sitting on the bench and Dvorak is in net tonight. The way things are, people are going to get hurt, and it would crush me if he was one of them. I only see him a few times when the camera focuses on the Quakes' bench. He looks like he wants to jump the boards and join the mix. When he was super young, he played D, and I can see him in that position. He has the build and speed for defense. Reading his expression, he wishes he were out there stapling someone to the boards. Play is fierce, with shots on goal by both teams, but no one is scoring. The temperature between the teams is rising so much I'm surprised the ice isn't melting.

I cheer when Luka strips the puck in our zone and skates strong for neutral ice. Number Five on the Liberty comes out of nowhere and checks him low to high, hard at center ice. The rising chest hit sends Luka's body airborne, and he loses his helmet from the impact of the illegal body strike. His head slams down first, followed by the rest of his body onto the ice, right in front of another Liberty skater who's too close to stop.

My hand covers my mouth as I watch, horrified. The player's skateblade slices diagonally across Luka's face. His gloved hands fly to his injury as he curls into a ball on the frozen surface. All the refs blow their whistles in unison. Any stick tapping that started on the Liberty bench in celebration of the hit peters out, replaced by a buzz of confusion in the stands.

A pool of blood forms beneath him, rapidly spreading. Our team's med staff jump the boards and rush to his side, sliding onto their knees to get to him. I stare at the high-def screen and see Linc rush out on the ice with them and crouch by Luka. He's staying out of the way but obviously talking to his friend from the way his lips are moving. Sonny does his captain thing and settles the Quakes on shift. Many of them have dropped their sticks and gloves, ready to tear apart the Liberty players at fault, their faces twisted in rage. The players on the bench, including Brian, rocket to their feet. Some are angry, but most have expressions of worry, horror, and concern etched on their faces.

The camera finds the Liberty player whose skate did the damage. His stunned expression communicates a deep, profound grief. He numbly allows his captain to skate him off the ice and disappears down the tunnel.

"Jess, that was a clean hit, in my opinion, just bad timing. We sure hope Ribic is okay," some asshole sports announcer rattles off, filling time while they wheel the stretcher out on the ice. *What the fuck? Who gives a shit about the hit?* There's way too much blood on the ice.

His co-host seems to agree with me. She stumbles to answer as they replay the horrible moment when Luka must see the skate coming because he curls away. He can't move fast enough to avoid the thirty-five-mile-an-hour knife blade hurtling toward him. "That young man will be lucky not to lose an eye. I think the hit is the last thing the team cares about." *You fucking moron* was left unsaid, but I said it for her. Shouted it, actually.

I blindly reach for my cell on the couch beside me and

dial. "Dad, I know Mom didn't want you watching the games, so I need to tell you—"

"I saw it, Catie. Your mother is already reaching out to the top plastic surgeon in the area and the best sports ophthalmologists we can find. We're taking care of our boy, don't worry. I'll tell you what we find out."

"Oh, Dad, it was so awful," I whisper as they cut to a shot of Luka, still in full gear with most of his face swathed in pressure bandages. Blood is still seeping out as he's loaded into an ambulance.

The ambulance that waits outside of every game because, as I just witnessed, things on the ice can change in a heartbeat, and then any chance to say you're sorry is gone.

"Anything can happen to anyone, on and off the ice, Catie. That's a lesson I think we've all been reminded of." His tone is gentle, and I guess he's trying to comfort me, but they've brought out shovels and buckets to scoop the frozen blood off the surface. His words about disaster happening to anyone, combined with the gruesome visual in the deathly silent arena, send chills down my spine.

The sports commentators continue filling air space, talking about other horrible injuries from skate blades, including wrists, eyes, and necks that changed lives. The Referee skates to center ice after the video huddle to make his call. "Five-minute major and game misconduct number Five, charging." The Liberty fans boo the call as their player is forced to leave the game. He deserves that and more. Hopefully, the NHL Player Safety Commission suspends his ass for the rest of the season. Sadly, he'll probably only get a slap on the hand and a single-game suspension.

As the teams face off at center ice, the camera catches Linc's grim expression from his spot back on the bench. Dressed to step in, he couldn't have gone to the hospital even if they'd let him. His job is to be there in case Raki gets injured, and so he has to stay, no matter how much it seems to physically hurt him. He grabs a towel and wipes what looks like blood and tears off his face.

Right then and there, I decide I'm going to fix this thing between us, no matter what it takes.

X

It's Monday, the day of our last away game of the season, and Dad arrives at the team offices for the first time since his heart attack. Since he's still technically in charge, his spacious corner office has been empty. Now it's filled with warm greetings, laughs, and thank yous to all the support staff who came to congratulate him on his return. When everyone clears the room, I hug him and hold on, unwilling to let go. It wasn't long ago I feared I'd never get to do this again. Once we part, he gestures me to the couch. Sitting, we angle toward each other, and I take him in.

He looks fantastic. There's color back in his cheeks, and even though it's obvious he's lost some weight, he's still robust. A bit of heaviness lifts from my shoulders. Now, if only the crushing sadness and heartache would go away, I, too, would feel like myself again. I'm not sure if that will ever happen. When I set out to hurt Linc, I crushed him and myself.

"I talked with Coach this morning." Dad's been letting me handle more and more, so I figure he's looking for an update on Luka and the team. No reason for both of us to tag team O'Ryan. "Luka is doing well, but he isn't going to be able to come home until later this week. The good news is that the surgery on his eyelid has been a success. They won't know for sure until it heals, but the doctor is optimistic his vision will be unaffected. Especially when the corneal swelling resolves."

"That's fantastic, so why the hold? He'll heal better here in California among friends."

"It's the concussion from where his head impacted the ice.

It's a grade 3. Plus, the doctors want the delicate facial sutures to settle more before he travels to minimize scarring." I frown. "He's out for the rest of the season, obviously. Mostly from the severe concussion, which only time will tell how fast he'll recover from. It could be anywhere from three to six months. The stitches might come out as early as next week."

"How's his mental health?"

A sigh escapes. "Not great. He's not talking to anyone. If asked a direct question, he'll answer, but other than that…" Not only do I feel horrible for Luka, but for his friends as well. "Coach has spoken with him, but he refuses to answer any calls from his teammates."

"Again, when he gets home, the team will surround him and support him, whether he wants them to or not. It's early days." Dad gives my knee a comforting squeeze. "How are the boys handling all of this?"

I don't know if Luka was the inspiration to end the game quickly, but in the third period, Brian broke the tie by scoring twice, winning the game for the Quakes. "They got to the hospital as soon as possible, but no one was allowed to see him. The mood on the plane Sunday morning heading to Boston from Philadelphia was intense, according to Coach. None of them wanted to leave their teammate behind. He decided on an off-ice team-building exercise that afternoon. He took them to the Commons for group drills, then it was a soccer scrimmage."

"I saw. A lot of Boston Beacon fans came out. There are videos all over social media."

"Yeah, Josh will be happy." I look down at my clenched hands in my lap and realize my fingers are turning white. Expecting my father to ask if Coach thinks the boys are fit to play tonight. I'm aware of how quiet the room has gotten. I can't look up and meet his gaze. Between my heartbreak and worrying about Linc and how he's taking Luka's injury, I haven't been sleeping. My dad is smart and observant, and there's only so much makeup can do to hide the dark circles that have taken residency under my eyes since our split.

"Catherine," he speaks my name with tenderness and love. My head tilts upward, and I meet his concerned gaze. "Don't think for a moment, even with my illness, I haven't noticed. You're miserable. Talk to me, Catiebug."

Shit. I've been trying so hard not to add to his stress, even before his heart attack, but somehow, he still manages to keep his finger on the pulse. "It seems silly, with everything that's been going on, but…I, um…broke it off with Linc."

The room goes quiet, and the silence stretches again as he stares at me. *Ugh*. He's waiting for me to fill the gap. I hate it when he does this. So, I give him the most obvious excuse. "Stop looking at me that way. I had to. As the first woman NHL owner, I can't have the bad optics of sleeping with a player."

"Catherine, we both know you're lying. Why don't you tell me the truth?"

"Dad." If Daniel finds out, Linc's career is over. "I-I can't." I won't let that happen. It's the whole reason there's a hole in my chest where my heart belongs.

"You broke things off with Linc, the love of your life, to protect him." My jaw drops, and my eyes grow round. How the hell did he find out? Dad chuckles and, with a finger under my chin, helps me close my mouth. "Sweetheart, I *always* notice if there's something wrong with *any* of my children, which includes Daniel. And, of course, Josh, but he's always the easiest of you three."

"Daniel's troubled, he's sick. I don't know how to help him. I don't even recognize him anymore."

"Luckily, I do." His lips thin, and sadness fills his blue eyes. "I tracked him down on Sunday, and your mother and I had a heart-to-heart with him."

"Oh, thank God. Is he going to be okay?"

"He will be. His problems stretch back to some sketchy

investments in the stock market, which took a dive. Then he resorted to gambling, hoping to win enough money to set him straight, which, of course, didn't work. In turn, he started drinking and acting like an asshole, driving Shannon to divorce him."

"I had no idea." I still feel guilty for not noticing he was in trouble sooner.

"None of us did. He became much better at hiding things than we ever gave him credit for. It is what it is." He shrugs. "Anyway, we had a good talk, and then he told your mom and me about blackmailing you to break it off with Linc."

"I'm sorry, Dad. You've been so stressed with work, and then you had a heart attack. I couldn't bring this to you."

"I know Catie. You only wanted to protect me. But I'm your father. It's part of my job description to look after my children." He smiles. "Daniel entered a rehab program yesterday."

"Oh, wow, that's fantastic. I should visit him or call."

"You can't, not for a while. Eventually, he'll be allowed phone calls and then in-person visits, but for now, he's cut off from the world."

That has to be tough for both him and our family. We've always been close. But if this is what he needs to get better and return to his old self, it will be worth the separation. I only hope he puts in the effort.

He takes my hand in both of his. "And now for you. First, your mother and I, um, let's say 'strongly encouraged' Daniel to destroy Rainbow's fake confession. It's gone and out of play. Knowing that, what do you want?"

"Oh, Dad. I want Linc. I always have. But you have no idea…I had to make sure he wouldn't fight for us, had to obliterate any feelings he had for me. He'll never forgive me."

"He might not." He squeezes my hand as an ache settles deep in my chest. "Linc called me Friday."

"He did?"

"He asked to be traded. He's set on moving back to Minnesota." My free hand flies to cover my mouth, and my heart breaks all over again. It's too late. "Stop. Whatever you're thinking right now, stop."

I wrench from my dad's hold and leap to my feet. "You don't get it. Ever since Luka's injury, I've tried to talk to Linc, calling, texting, but he's blocked my number, so I can't even leave a message. I destroyed us..." I want to run from the room, run from the horrible situation I created, but my name from my father's lips holds me in place.

"Catherine." My dad stands and grips my shoulders. "You are a fucking Bishop, so act like one. I didn't become a self-made billionaire by giving up. And you're not the first female NHL owner by not working hard. Yes, I'm handing the reins over to you, but you earned it. If I thought you weren't the best person for this job, I wouldn't be giving you control. What have I taught you?"

"There's *always* a solution for every problem," I mumble half-heartedly.

"That's right. I told him I won't trade him, so he's planning on retiring. It's going to be announced before Saturday's game." He squeezes my shoulder. "So, what are you going to do?"

My mind spins. He's right, there *is* a solution to every problem, and I am my father's daughter. And then it comes to me. I know just the epic miracle to hopefully do the trick. It's a long shot, but I'm willing to aim for the back of the net. I'm going to play a two-hundred-foot game. My smile is almost a grin.

"That's my girl. What can I do to help?"

CHAPTER
Twenty-One

LINCOLN

I'm taking my time changing into my suit. We squeaked by the Colorado Heights, snagging the win, two-one. Thank God. Monday's game against Boston sucked ass. It was my first loss in a while. I'll take the blame for letting the pucks pass me, but the whole team played like shit. Sluggish skating, turnovers, and missed passes were gifts to the Beacons, who took every advantage. And why not? They are number one in the league, setting new NHL records this season. There's a reason for their success.

Tonight's game was shaping up to be a repeat of Mondays, but as we were about to hit the ice for warm-ups, Coach told us the good news that Luka would be flying home on Friday. Spirits lifting, the team was almost back to form. For once, I was glad to be riding the bench. My mind is in turmoil between Luka, who's not taking any of our calls, and my two conversations with Robert Bishop.

My first chat with the owner of the Quakes didn't go as expected. He got me to spill my guts. He told me I could retire because he wouldn't trade me, intent on this crazy notion that it's ride or die, wanting me to be a Quake for life since this is the only team I've ever played for. But he made me promise not to make any plans past that. Bishop wanted time to get to the bottom of things. And he did.

I was in my hotel room Sunday night in Boston when he called. He explained how he'd confronted Daniel and found out he blackmailed Catherine into burning our relationship to the ground in order to protect me. I think he hoped I'd magically lose my hurt and anger, forgiving her, but I disappointed him.

I know at the start of the season, I was dead set against retiring, even though I felt broken and old. But now I'm healthier and playing some of my best tending in my career. However, I realized Tolli was right. I've accomplished a lot during my time on the ice. I've won two Cups, a Vezina Trophy, and was nominated for the Hart Memorial Trophy. Plus, Raki and I are in the mix for the Jennings Trophy, the tandem team allowing the fewest goals in the regular season, even with my earlier bad form. There's not much more for me to do. If Robert won't trade me so I can be part of building another team as a player, I'm okay with finally retiring.

Of course, he had to push the Quakes' player development position. I told him it would be too hard to work for the organization and see Catherine every day. He made an enticing pitch, pushing the fact she was only trying to protect me. By the end of the call, we agreed they would announce my retirement at Saturday's game.

I promised him I'd think things through as far as leaving L.A. My problem is twofold—I can't concentrate until I see Luka, so thinking about Catherine hasn't been a priority. Zach, Brian, and I have been worried sick. Normally, you can't get the chatty little fuck to stop yammering on, so it's upsetting that he won't speak to any of us. According to Coach, the doc saved his eye, and he'll be good to play next season. It's a drag to miss the playoffs, but not enough for this disappearing act to make any sense. Something else is going on under that perfectly coiffed hair of his. At least when he gets home, there'll be no hiding from us or, hell, the team. We will have his back and get him through this.

Just like I would have had Catherine's back if she had only talked to me. It doesn't seem that she thinks of the two of us as a team the way I do. Deep down, I know she was trying to do what she thought was best for me, and if our situation was reversed, I can't honestly say I wouldn't have done the same. But why didn't she come to me? We could have handled Daniel's blackmail together. I think I'm more hurt knowing she didn't trust me enough to keep my shit together. I don't know if I can get past it or not.

"Hey," Brian taps me on the shoulder. "Stop with the deep thoughts. Luka's coming home. We need to celebrate."

"Yeah, you're right." I rustle up a smile I'm not feeling.

"I forgot to tell you. Phoebe came to the game tonight. She's waiting in the lounge. She's going to come with us to MacKay's."

"Cool, man. I haven't seen Pheebs in forever." We head out of the locker room behind Holt as Zach joins us. "How's she adjusting to the move?"

"Good. She's still looking for work, but I told her not to stress. It's not like I can't support her."

Zach laughs. "True that."

As we enter the lounge, a feminine shriek fills the air. Matt breaks into a run, leaving us in the dust. With the kind of speed he's known for on the ice, he arrives in time to catch a brunette before she faceplants on the floor. It's Phoebe who looks into Holt's eyes with a mix of innocence, gratitude, and mischief that only Bri's baby sister can carry off. We rush to her side as Holt sets her on her feet, keeping a steadying hand on her shoulder since she's wearing pencil-thin high heels. Who wears shoes like that to a hockey game, especially since she is dressed in jeans and is wearing Brian's jersey?

"What the hell, Pheebs? What were you doing?" Brian glares at her, and she laughs.

She smiles and points to one of the framed photos of the team through the years on the wall above the couch. "I wanted a closer look. I love that one of you guys with the Cup, and well, you know me." She shrugs and giggles.

"Yeah, you're a freaking klutz, so why in the world did you think it's a good idea to stand on the couch in heels?"

"I'm fine, Bri." Phoebe hugs him and turns to Matt, who's still standing by her side. "Hey, big dude, thanks for the assist."

Holt blinks and almost smiles. "You're welcome. You might want to stay off couches."

She grins. "Then where will I eat dinner when watching TV?"

"He means standing on them, sis." Brian takes her hand. "Come on, trouble, let's get out here before you cause another disaster." He gives a chin lift to Holt before escorting Phoebe from the lounge.

"Good save, Holt." I acknowledge, only to find him staring at Phoebe's ass as she exits, completely ignoring me. Zach notices as well. Alrighty then. I shrug and follow Brian out, with Zach by my side.

X

A couple of beers in at MacKay's, and I am so regretting that I told my dickhead friends and Pheebs the truth of why Catherine dumped me.

"So, wait a minute," Phoebe ponders. "Now that you know she was trying to keep you from being crucified on social media by these bullshit lies of Rainbow's, and you're still mad at her?"

"Well, yeah, she should have come to me. Unless she thought it was true."

"She did a Sydney Carton and stepped to the guillotine for you, and you have the balls to be pissed?" Bri sounds incredulous and kind of nerdy, if I'm being honest.

"Who the fuck is that? Do you mean Sydney Crosby?"

He shakes his head and swears. "Pick up a classic sometime, shithead, instead of all your thrillers. How about she's your Obi-Wan who let Vader cut him down so Luke can live? Do you think Luke was pissed at the old man for that?"

"No, it's way closer to the song *The Highwayman* by Loreena McKennitt," Zach says in his lilting Swedish accent. When we stare back blankly at him, he gives a mournful sigh. "Oh man, how do you guys not know that song or the poem it's based on?"

"The one about the black-eyed daughter of the guy running an inn who sacrifices her life to warn her lover, a highwayman, that the cops are waiting for him? I love that song," Phoebe says as she clasps her hands with a doe-eyed expression, "such a tragedy. She wants to be with him but would rather die than see him in jail or dead." Zach clinks his beer to her wineglass, and they grin at each other.

I sip my beer, looking at the two aliens who have taken over my friends and, apparently, Pheebs as well. "This is the weirdest conversation I've ever had."

"Fine, let's leave the comps out of it for now," Bri signals the rookie to get more beer for our table. "Here's the only thing you have to ask yourself—how does the thought of living without her make you feel?"

"Like crap," I reply without hesitation. "But living with her and never knowing who the real Cat is, if she's going to blindside me again with another one-eighty change of plans without even talking to me? That shit makes me feel like I'm free falling off a cliff into a big black pit."

"Is there anything she can do to convince you her love is

real?" Sonny asks. Is there a twinkle in his eyes? Can't be. He's not enough of a dick to get amusement from my misery. Or maybe I don't know anyone anymore?

"I'm not sure, bud. If there is, I can't imagine what it could be." Desperate to get their attention off my love life, I see Holt sitting isolated on a picnic bench with a couple of other young guns who ignore his grumpy ass. He's been staring at Pheebs all evening. "You know who really needs help? Young Matthew Holt seems to have been bitten by the Phoebe bug today. Look at that poor bastard. He's totally smitten."

"The hell he is," Brian growls. "He better not. Or I'll personally introduce him to the hockey bro code—sisters are out of bounds. Anyone on a team knows this."

"Don't be such a caveman," Phoebe chides, giving her big bro a playful punch to the arm. "We already have one of those, and one is quite enough. Besides, I think he's kind of cute." Bri catches her shooting Holt a flirtatious smile and clenches his fist.

Sonny and I crack up, waving to a confused and kind of pissed off looking Holt. Shit, he probably thinks we're laughing at him. Stopping pucks is fucking hard, and yet it seems like a piece of cake compared to all this emotional stuff I'm wading through. Maybe I should rethink retiring and stick to keeping fifty pounds of gear between the rest of the world and me. I seem fated to keep fucking it up.

My heart wants to forgive her, but my head says to steer clear. I feel like I'm in limbo. Right now, I have no plans for what I'm doing after the playoffs. I don't know what to do about Catherine. Could the Universe, for once, do me a fucking favor and give me a sign? Because I feel pretty fucking clueless.

X

W arm-ups started earlier than normal, agreed upon with Anaheim, so the Quakes can do my retirement announcement. I stand in my crease while my team and the Magics line the boards. The lights dim in the stadium, and then a spotlight isolates me when the usual music bumper for a Quakes' promo video fills the arena. The monitors light with a montage of me making saves starts to play.

The announcer comes over the speakers. "Okay, Quakes' fans, tonight we honor our two-time Cup-winning goalie, Lincoln Cavanaugh." Cheers thunder from the audience. "Number Thirty-Three is officially retiring at the end of this season, and this is his last regulation game." The fan reaction is a mixture of supportive cheers and cries of "Nooooo."

I raise my stick in salute while both teams give me stick taps.

"So we have a couple of special messages for you, Caveman. Take it away, Stewie!"

The jumbotrons, which were playing game highlights of my career, are now filled with Stewie from *The Family Guy*, dressed as a goalie standing in his crease. Only instead of having himself on his helmet like mine, he has a cartoon of me. I laugh and shake my head. Holy cow, how'd they get this made in time? It's Saturday, and I only told Robert I was retiring last Friday. Wow, Seth MacFarlane and his team rock.

Then my heart breaks a little bit more. The only person who knows the Stewie story other than my family and my guys—and I doubt Josh and his team reached out to them—is Catherine. Fucking A, I had to block her number to stop her barrage of texts and messages. Is she pulling on my heartstrings or using personal information to further promote what's about to be her team and sell more tickets next year? Thousands of phones in the stands are videoing this. The retweets alone will get a ton of views, which means more free advertising. But soon, the cartoon banishes the bleak thoughts from my mind.

"Hello, Los Angeles Quakes." Stewie's upper-crust British accent has his usual snobby emphasis. "So, your tiny goalie at 6'4" and two hundred pounds has done a pretty decent job. Good thing, or I'd have to eliminate him." He pulls a laser gun out from behind his back and fires it a few times. *God, wouldn't that be handy to have during a game?* Then he goes on about my career accomplishments of Stanley Cup wins, the Vezina Trophy, and my lifetime stats. "Since he's graciously decided to walk away instead of fighting me for his position, victory is mine!"

His evil chuckle has the fans clapping. "Now listen up, Cavanaugh," heavy on the sneer when he says my name, "someone has a special message just for you."

Stewie disappears, and Catherine takes his place. I can't tell where she is, whether this is pre-recorded or live, but my heart starts pumping at seeing her again. My stomach flips, and my throat closes as emotions swamp me. God, I miss her. No matter what her motivation for doing this, I can't take my eyes off the screen.

"On behalf of the Quakes, we want to thank you for everything you've done for this team and community. Lincoln, you are a forever Quake and a part of this family." She pauses and swallows hard before looking directly into the camera and straight into my soul. "On a personal note, I'd like to ask for your forgiveness. I'm an idiot, and I'm so sorry. There is no excuse, except perhaps caring too much. I love you, Lincoln Cavanaugh."

There is a collective "Aww" from the uncharacteristically quiet crowd. And then the stick taps start from my boys and soon spread to the Magic as well.

Holy shit! She announced her feelings in front of a sold-out crowd of over eighteen thousand. I stare at the monitor, transfixed. "Forgive me?" She lifts a stuffed Stewie and kisses him.

When her lips press on his oversized baldhead, the arena is flooded with light. First one, then two stuffed Stewies hit the ice. Soon, the air is filled with them, and they are flooding the ice like a crazy hat trick gone wild. They keep coming. There must be hundreds of them.

The stands burst out in cheers, and their stomping feet rock the barn. There are some hoots and catcalls. The organist gets in the act and plays some freakin' love song that I recognize but can't name. I laugh and look toward the owner's box, but there's no way I can see her through the glaring lights. My head balks a little, but my heart overrules it, and I do the only thing I can think of. Pulling off my glove, my fingers first touch my heart and then my lips. Finally, I blow her a kiss. The cheers escalate to a whole other level.

The ice crew comes out with bags and bins, scooping the Stewies off the ice as the announcer states all the dolls will be donated to charity. With the epic grand gesture over, it's time for the fun to begin. I'm revved and ready to play my last game of regular season hockey.

X

Sweat drips into my eye. I shake my head, clearing the biting drops as I peer around the hulking body of an opposing team member, trying to find the puck. The arena is loud. Always is with our freeway rivals. Especially when we're in the final minutes of the game as the clock counts down. Our team is trying to clear our zone, but Anaheim is giving it their all, trying to get a point on the board. The Magic's captain snipes a shot at my net. The blistering puck heads my way until, out of nowhere, Holt appears. He manages to block the biscuit with his stick, sending it to the boards. With a hard crunch, Connor pins a Magic to the boards while Holt skates in and snags the puck. Matt sends the puck to the neutral zone, perfectly placing the disc to Brian's tape after he jumped the boards, leaving the bench. Bri doesn't miss a stride, hustling to the O-zone. He jigs a defensive man, and then it's just him and their goalie.

Brian takes the shot, and doing what the Quakes' lead scorer does, gets the puck inside the net. The goal buzzer sounds and our fans are on their feet. After Brian's celly and fist bumps to the bench, we set for the puck drop at center ice. I glance at the clock to see there's only twenty seconds left of play. The Ref drops the puck, and Anaheim wins the draw. I crouch, making myself huge in my net as the Magic players are fast-passing the puck. The screen in front of me sucks, so I give a shove to the Anaheim player standing too close, and I hear a *crack* of a slap shot. With the opposing player out of the way, I see the puck heading to the opposite corner of my goal from me. I lunge, doing the splits as I raise my glove. *Smack*. The puck slaps my glove, and I throw myself forward, not wanting momentum, carrying my glove past the line. Laying on the ice, with the biscuit safe in my glove, the end game buzzer blares. Game over, and we won, five to zero. I have another career shutout for my record. Fucking yeah. I jump up while throwing my stick, glove, and blocker in the air and take my helmet off, dropping it on the ice.

All the players and coaches flood onto the ice in a wave. I glance to the owner's box, but the familiar face I'm looking for I only get a glimpse before Bri, Sonny, and even Holt are dogpiling on top of me to celebrate the victory. It's a mass of sweaty, smelly dudes, and the emotion hits me hard how much I'm going to miss this. Thank God there are the playoffs.

As my team, coaches, and staff let me up for air, I notice the Anaheim Magics are still on the ice, standing in a line. Wow, usually, after a loss, the opposing players hightail it back to the locker room. I swallow hard and skate forward, reaching their team captain first.

"Cavanaugh," he shakes my hand. "Can't say I'm going to

miss you being in net, you large son of a bitch. Congratulations."

"Thanks, man."

I work my way through the line as the Magics show their respect for my career. It's sort of surreal since our teams can't stand each other. I reach their goalie and backup.

"Dude, we've got one less American goalie with you retiring." He shakes my hand and pulls me into a hug. "You had a hell of a career. Hopefully, I can follow in your footsteps."

"You can try, Davidson." We laugh. He's young and cocky enough to probably do it.

Anaheim leaves the ice, and my team surrounds me at center ice, tapping their sticks while the crowd cheers. I wave and spin in a circle, acknowledging the fans, when I spot her. Catherine, in skates, with a Stewie doll in hand, has joined the team's circle. She's wearing my jersey. My name and number are displayed for all to see.

Overcome, I skate to her, heft her in my arms, and kiss her as we spin in a circle less graceful than a figure skater but more controlled than a fight. She laughs. The kiss develops into a deep, sizzling one that earns cat-calls from the players and thousands of fans still glued to their seats. Finally, I place her on her skates but keep my hands on her hips.

"Does this mean I'm forgiven?" Cat actually looks a bit worried.

I stare right into her eyes. "Promise me one thing."

"Anything."

"Never leave me."

"Even if you decide to move back to Minnesota, I'm with you always."

"When everything I want is right here?" I snort in reply. "That was a brief bit of insanity. I think your dad played us."

She laughs. "Of course he did. He's a big romantic and a huge manipulator.

"I love you, Catherine Bishop."

"I love you, Lincoln Cavanaugh." She grins as tears stream down her cheeks.

I yank her close and move my hands so they clasp her face, and I kiss her for a long, long time. The crowd still in the building goes wild again, even louder this time as the Quakes' victory song, *Hollywood Nights,* by Bob Seger, blares through the arena again. Yeah, I'm feeling pretty lucky right now. I may not know what the future has in store for us, but the one thing I know is I will never let go of her again.

Epilogue

LINCOLN

"I got him, I got him!" Bransom, one of this year's draft picks, bellows out as he puts on the burners chasing down an opponent in the last scrimmage game of development camp. There's a resounding *crack* as Einar Kuznetsov lets loose with an amazing slapshot that…booms against the glass a mile from the net.

"Silky," one of his teammates barks out with a laugh.

"I was aiming for the rafters," he jokes back.

Tolli and I, each coaching our own teams, grin at each other before he calls out, "Let's go boys, hustle out there, can't have Cavey's crew beat us."

"Again," I add with a smirk.

The play is intense but also joyful. I really like the goalie prospect on my scrimmage team. He's talented and a talker—to the pucks. His shouts of "Too close" and "Got you" when he makes a save, cracks me up. All the players are beaming, having so much Goddamn fun out there, learning and building their confidence. Even though I didn't get to take off as much time this summer as I usually do, I'm still having a blast. It's July, and my first rookie development as part of the staff is winding down to the final minutes.

It's the first time I've been to one of these camps since I was eighteen or nineteen, the same age as most of the kids on the ice today. I'm loving it so much I kind of wish I'd taken the time to help out during the off season years ago. Then again, camping and fishing with my family was the mental break I needed from the daily stress of being a pro, so I probably wouldn't have had as much fun. It's a great group of kids, including our most recent draft picks, returning college draft players, and rookies from our farm team, the Ontario Tsunami, who I feel a few will get called up this coming season. There are also a few invitees who weren't in the draft but on our scout's radar.

After today's session, Tolli, the trainers, and I will review the videos and discuss a game plan for the fall. When September rolls around, it'll be the Quakes' training camp getting ready for the start of the season. All the players will need to prove they deserve a spot on the team. While we won't be directly involved in training, Tolls likes to watch and see if any of the younger players need special attention we can help with. Between now and training camp, we have a group vacation planned to the Caribbean. It'll be Bri, along with his sister Phoebe, Sonny and his wife Jenny, and Cat and I. I can't wait to hit the resort. We tried to get Luka to come with us, but he refused.

He's being a stubborn asshole. After he came home from the hospital, Luka managed to keep dodging us, but we finally caught him at the team's gym. Cat gave security the okay for me to search the off-hour access log, and that's when I found he'd been working out after midnight. He's there for a couple of hours and then leaves. I guess he's having trouble sleeping because when we confronted him, he looked like shit.

And I'm not talking about the angry red scar slashing diagonally across his face from hairline to neck. There's only so much even the best Bishop-level money paid for plastic surgeon could do. The doc promised him it would fade and not be so pronounced, but he will wear his wound for life. More concerning are the shadows under his eyes and he's lost weight. All of us are worried about him, but at least after we confronted him at the gym, he's speaking to us again. However, getting him to hang out is like keeping Holt out of the penalty box. Mostly, we go to his place because he won't be seen in public. He claims the one time he hit the grocery store, he scared a kid. Now he has his food delivered.

The good news about Luka is at the beginning of July, he cleared the concussion protocol. He can start skating again and get back to his full fitness routine. Though physically, his life can get back to normal, we're all worried about his mental health. His family in Slovenia wanted to visit as soon as they knew he was injured, but he told them to stay home. His mother, Maja, ignored him and came right after his release. She spent a week with him before she had to return home. That's probably the only reason he's talking to anyone. Mama Maja is a force to be reckoned with.

His concussion was pretty bad back then, so he doesn't remember much of the Quakes' run for the Cup. The team made it all the way to game seven of round three. We battled to the bitter end trying to make the finals, but it wasn't in our cards, and we lost to the Chicago Storm. I cheered for the Washington Red Tails when they beat the Storm in four games, sweeping the Stanley Cup. If the Quakes couldn't have it, sure as shit, I wouldn't root for the team who knocked us out of contention.

The whistle to end the scrimmage game blows, and I'm

pulled from my thoughts as the kids skate toward the benches. They take a knee on the ice in a semicircle around us. Coach O'Ryan is in front, having watched the last day of camp.

"Good job this week. I've heard great things about all of you from the development staff." The players hoot and holler. A few tap their sticks. "You've all been given your personal game plan on what to work on, along with exercise and nutrition programs. When I see a bunch of you in September, there better be improvement."

Some of these kids will be going back to college, others to their home countries to play in their professional leagues. But some will be here in a couple of months to prove themselves, trying their hardest to make a place for themselves on their first NHL team. Some might achieve it, but more likely, they'll play for the Tsunami, where they'll continue to learn their game and develop their bodies. I'm rooting for each and every one of them, and I'm excited to be a part of their journey.

X

I'm showered and changed into a T-shirt and cargo shorts, tossing my damp towel into the bin before exiting the locker room. Unlocking my phone, I notice I don't have any calls or texts from Cat. She was supposed to see Daniel today. I'm sort of split in my feelings. On the one hand, he's her brother, and they used to be close, so I'd like for their relationship to improve. But on the other, I'm not a fan. If Daniel were out of the picture, I'd be a happy guy. Which, of course, I'd never tell Catherine. All I want for her is her happiness, and if reconnecting with her asshole brother brings a gorgeous smile to her face, then I'm behind her one hundred percent.

I turn the corner and halt. At the far end of the hall is the sexy new owner of the Quakes. She's wearing a sundress and strappy flat sandals as she talks with Coach O'Ryan. I take a moment to admire her before she spots me. She's beautiful. Her mocha skin glows, and her long, dark hair is pulled into a high ponytail. I wish her dress was shorter because my woman has amazing legs. But it's her smile and laughter which hits me the most. I love how happy she is.

She spots me, and her smile shapes into a grin. When I reach her side, I place a kiss on her temple before acknowledging the man at her side.

"Hey, Coach."

"Not your coach anymore, Lincoln. You can call me, Tim."

I shake my head. "Never gonna happen. You'll always be Coach to me."

He laughs. "I know you've hung up your goalie skates, but I hope you'll mentor your replacement we got during free agency."

The Quakes got Olivier Roy from the Toronto Ice. He's looking for more play, wanting a tandem or second goalie post, which he wasn't getting with the Ice. When he stepped in a few times last season because their main tendy got injured, Olly put up some outstanding stats. We were lucky we could afford him.

"Of course. Anything for the Quakes."

"Good answer." He turns to Catherine. "I'm looking forward to the season. We'll catch up more later." He says his goodbyes and leaves.

"Hey beautiful, how was your visit?" I place my hands on her hips and pull her closer. Her dark brown eyes shine with happiness.

"It went great. Daniel is doing so well. It's like I have my brother back."

"I'm happy for you." I drop a kiss on her lips, loving I can

PDA whenever I want now. "I wasn't expecting you. You've got plans?"

"I sure do. I'm taking my hot hockey boyfriend out to lunch."

"Hot, huh?"

"Yup. He's got the best ass in the league." I scrunch my forehead, not expecting her reply, though I know she has a thing for my butt. "It's a thing," she laughs. "You know, out of all the sports, hockey players have the finest asses."

I wind my hand through her silky hair and give it a gentle tug as I laugh. "How many sports butts have you studied? I never pay much attention, so I'll have to take your word for it."

"It's true, trust me. And if you play your cards right, there might be a personal celebration at my house for your first successful rookie development camp."

"Hmm," I wrap my arm around her shoulder, tucking her in close as I lead us outside. "That certainly sounds like an incentive."

"Like we need the incentive to get naked." She curls her arm around my waist, holding me tight, just the way I like it.

Who would have thought I would be here? Earlier this season, I thought my life was crashing and burning. And these days, I can't ask for anything more. Now, I just need to figure out when and how to propose to this woman. She's my everything. She holds my heart and soul. My future looks bright, indeed.

X

Thanks for reading, *Lincoln*. Please consider leaving a review. If you'd like more Linc and Catherine, scan the QR code on the next page for a bonus scene.

Next Up is Luka Ribic. After suffering a horrific injury during a game, can beauty heal the beast? Scan the QR code below.

The Los Angeles Quakes

The Los Angeles Quakes
    Goalie: Alexandr Dvorak ("Raki")—(Russian)—#31
    Goalie: Lincoln Cavanaugh ("Caveman/Cavie")—(American)—#33
    Goalie: Olivier Roy ("Olly")—(Canadian)—#35

1st Line:
    Center: Zach Hansson ("Sonny")—Captain (Swedish)—#10
    Right-wing: Connor D'Angelo ("Clutch")—(American)—#9
    Left-wing: Luka Ribic ("Ribi")—(Slovenian)—#20
    Defensemen: Matthew "Matt" Holt ("Mattie"/ "Holtie")—(America)—#5
    Defensemen: Edouard Landry ("Eddie")—Alternate Captain (French Canadian)—#22

2nd Line:
    Center: Brian Anderson ("Bri")—Alternate Captain (American)—#13
    Right-Wing: Michael Cote ("Mikey")—(Canadian)—#19

Left-Wing: Cory Fournier ("Foursie")—(French Canadian)—#24

Defensemen: Alex Bouchard ("Bouch")—(French Canadian)—#4

Defensemen: Anzor Zaytseva ("Z")—(Chechen Republic)—#28

3rd Line:
Center: Jacob Novak ("Jake"/"Novi")—(American)—#41
Right-Wing: Andre Forsberg ("Bergie")—(Swedish)—#17
Left-Wing: Benjamin Kivi ("Kivi")—(Finland)—#25
Defensemen: Trevor Rayne ("Trev")—(American)—#23
Defensemen: Olek Popova ("Poppy")—(Ukrainian)—#77

4th Line:
Center: Nathan Russo ("Rue") —(American)—#18
Right-Wing: Axel Pedersen ("Axe")—(Norway)—#14
Left-Wing: Patrik Eklund ("Eeks")—Rookie (Swedish)—#50

Extra D:
Defensemen: Sean Baker ("Bakes")—Rookie (Canadian)—#44

Defensemen: Karl Nilsson ("Nilie")—(Swedish)—#6

About the Author

Alisa Jean is the pseudonym for award-winning authors Marla A. White and C J Bahr. They first teamed up over thirty years ago over a bottle of Zima (don't ask) while polishing their gear for a horse show. They've since moved on to better beverages and writing novels.

Separately, Marla prefers to murder characters in the usual way while C J uses paranormal means. The long-time best friends joined together as a writing team through their mutual love of hockey. Wonder twin powers activated! Their hockey romances examine flawed characters with heart, humor, and sexy sizzle.

> alisajean.author@gmail.com
> https://www.alisajean.com

- facebook.com/61567301825132
- instagram.com/alisajean.author
- bookbub.com/authors/alisa-jean

Also by Alisa Jean

Luka: A Los Angeles Quakes Hockey Series, Book 2

Scan Me

Matthew: A Los Angeles Quakes Hockey Series, Book 3

Scan Me

Coming Soon

Brian

Connor

Trevor

Cory

Also by Marla A White

Mysteries
Framed For Murder
Cause For Elimination
Bloodstains & Candy Canes
The Starlight Mint Surprise Murder

Contemporary Fantasy
The Keeper Chronicles
The Angel By The Tower
The Angel At The Gate
The Angel In The Window
The Keeper Chronicles Box Set

Also by CJ Bahr

Supernatural Suspense

Valley Fever

Paranormal Romance

The Fire Chronicles

Walking Through Fire

Forged In Fire

Redeemed By Fire

MISC

31 Overlook Hotel: 31 Authors, One Hotel Of A Story